THE
MECHANICAL ANGEL

The
Mechanical Angel

HIS ADVENTURES AND ENTERPRISES
IN THE GLITTERING 1920'S

BY

DONALD FRIEDE

ALFRED A. KNOPF : New York

1 9 4 8

FOR PASCAL COVICI

CONTENTS

THE
MECHANICAL ANGEL

She was a very pretty girl, and she also happened to be extremely intelligent. But she never managed to develop a tolerance for the habit most people had of throwing names around. She would listen for a while to the talk of Tallu and Noel and Bea—or maybe to retold conversations with Kip and Kit and Bill—and then she would break her silence, speaking in a loud clear voice that somehow managed to cut through the talk around her.

"Did I ever tell you," she would say to no one in particular, "about my conversation with Gertrude Stein?"

There would be a solemn shaking of heads, and a silence among the people in her immediate neighborhood.

"It was very interesting," she would say. "I was walking my dog in Paris one day and suddenly I saw Gertrude Stein coming down the street towards me. She too was walking her dog, and when we came abreast, the two dogs started to circle and sniff each other. Naturally we both stopped. And then Gertrude Stein smiled at me and said: 'Your dog likes my dog.'"

She would look around the room happily, savoring the respectful attention she was getting. "I smiled at her too," she would say. "I nodded my head. 'Yes,' I said, 'he does.'"

I never met Gertrude Stein. But this is a book about the twenties, and no book dealing with that era would be complete without some mention of her name. So be it. She has now been mentioned. And that leaves me free to go on to other things, guided always by the fine moral lesson I learned from my pretty friend—a lesson I have never forgotten.

FROM
THE
GROUND
UP

*I*T WAS in the early fall of 1923 that I finally came to the regretful conclusion that business in the accepted and conventional sense was not for me—nor I for it. I assured myself that I had done my best to adapt myself to it, I reconstructed my abortive career in the three years since I had left Princeton in the spring of my first year there—eating as I did in sophomore commons by virtue of the fact that I had been at Yale the previous year, I never have been able to decide if I left in my freshman or in my sophomore year—I examined it soberly, and I said to hell with it. It was very obvious that I was getting exactly nowhere extremely fast.

There was good reason for my feeling this way. Those three years had been taken up with trying to make something out of nine successive jobs, and in not one of them had I progressed beyond the first stage of apprenticeship. It was quite possible, I told myself, that the fault lay in me. But I never did manage to convince myself completely on that point. There was always the possibility that a tenth job might be just the right one for me. The trouble was that I seemed to be running out of new fields to be conquered by. I put myself in the hands of a psychoanalyst.

I had, as a matter of fact, started my business life quite soberly, in the banking school of the Guaranty Trust Company. I do not remember who my classmates were, but I am sure that they are now safely ensconced behind sober desks in some branch or other of that estimable institution. I am sure that they are very happy about it too, and I envy them not at all. It was obvious to me after only a very few months of complete bewilderment that I was not cut out to be a banker.

It took me just a little longer than that to find out that I was no more cut out to be a bond salesman. In those lush days this was a job that was open to the sons of big patrons of big brokerage houses, and the house I went to work for was one of the biggest. And if my father's dealings with them had not been in the Jesse Livermore brackets, at least they had been respectably large. Besides which my cousin had his first seat on the Stock Exchange and was well on his way toward his second and third one—this last he bought in mid-August of 1929, and he paid a little over five hundred thousand dollars for it, thereby earning himself membership in a very exclusive if somewhat unhappy group.

Somehow being a bond salesman seemed like an excellent idea, and it certainly did not require the long training that had evidently been such an important part of becoming a banker. All you did, it seemed, was to supply yourself with a brief case, stuffed with prospectuses of the current bond issues being sponsored by the firm that employed you. Armed with this infallible ammunition, and well fortified with sales arguments that had been impressively presented by a most adept spellbinder, you set out to sell your wares.

4

The trouble was, I soon found out, that there were hundreds of other salesmen, all equally well supplied with equally glowing prospectuses of bond issues that were quite as alluring as the ones I was offering. In fact they seemed to be much more alluring than anything I was trying to sell. Certainly after I had sold all the bonds I could to my cousins and my aunts and my other relatives, and to as many of my friends as I could possibly induce to invest in anything to give me a helping hand, I came on the lean days. And they were very lean indeed. I had glutted my market and I could find no new ones to explore. There was a decent interval in which I was permitted to convince myself, and my employers, of this fact, and then I ceased to be a bond salesman. I have never once regretted this fact.

My next run was a very short one. I went to work for the American Express Company as a translator. I spoke French, German, and Russian fluently, and I had no trouble in passing the conversational briefing I was given. But the art of the interview had not then been brought to the high stage of perfection it was to achieve in later years, and within a week it was discovered that my use of these languages was limited to the fine prose of the great masters of literature and to polite, colloquial, or idiomatic conversations. I knew nothing about the specialized languages of business, and my attempt on my third day there to translate a complicated letter from a French manufacturer of heavy machinery was a ludicrous job. I solved the problem very simply: I never showed up there again.

I was to remember this experience many years later, and to realize how much things had changed in the intervening time. In 1943 I was suddenly transferred from my comfortable berth in the Air Corps to War Department Intelligence and ordered to Camp Ritchie in Maryland, a place so legendarily top-secret at the time that it was rumored that one poor soldier, with orders to report there at once, had wandered around Washington for days, begging people to tell him how to get to the place and being indignantly denied the information from all quarters. This was the language camp, and you had to speak at least two foreign languages fluently in order to get there. And my dossier stated that I spoke three of them. I had not been there very long when I was put to the test. In all three of the languages I boasted of knowing I underwent the most rigorous examinations I have ever experienced, oral ones first, and then written ones, and I was limp with fatigue when I finished my long afternoon with my French, German, and Russian inquisitors. And just as I was congratulating myself on having survived the ordeal I found myself being interrogated by yet another man. I couldn't figure out what he was driving at. There seemed to be no rhyme or reason in the casual questions he was asking me. It wasn't until much later that I realized that this last man was trying to check on my knowledge of English—a valuable precaution in view of the high percentage of refugees who could barely make themselves understood in English at this most incredible of camps.

It was shortly after the American Express Company and I parted company that I went into tobacco. There never was any good reason for this move except for the fact that one of my closest friends had recently become associated with the official trade journal of the tobacco industry. It was he who suggested that I get a job as a salesman for the American Tobacco Company. There was, he assured me, a great future in that organization. He arranged an appointment for me, I went to see the man he had spoken to, and I got the job. Or rather I was told I could have the job if I could pass the two obligatory tests that had to be undertaken first: I had to qualify for a commercial driving license and I had to memorize a speech of some two hundred and fifty words. I set about to meet these requirements.

The reason for the commercial license was that I was expected to cover my territory—every store that carried tobacco on Ninth, Tenth, and Eleventh Avenues as far uptown as Seventy-second Street—in a Ford coupé with its rumble seat removed and in its place a large storage compartment, on each side of which was painted an advertisement for Bull Durham, complete with bull and fence. I carried with me a piece of green felt and a small Sterno stove and a frying pan. The felt was to be set up in a very special way on the store counter, after which the stove was to be placed on it and lighted. Into the frying pan was to be sprinkled a liberal portion of Lucky Strike Tobacco, and I was to sauté it gently over the flame. All this was to be done in complete silence—that is if the irate proprietor had not already thrown me out of the place. And as the delicious fumes of the warmed tobacco came wafting out of the frying pan, I was to take the pan off the flame and wave it gently under the noses of the customers in the store. Then, and only then, was I to go into the speech I had so carefully memorized. "See," it began, "It's Toasted."

As I remember it I did this for three months, although I haven't the slightest idea of why I stuck it out so long. And when I finally left the American Tobacco Company it was not because I had fumbled my speech, or because I had used too much Sterno in my toasting process. It had something to do with a long, slow skid on wet car tracks and some crumpled fenders and a somewhat battered bull on the left side of my car.

But I stayed in tobacco for another year. This time, however, I was in the retail end of the business. The United Cigar Stores were in the midst of long and involved negotiations with the French government whereby they hoped to buy from them the exceedingly profitable French tobacco monopoly. Having done this, they then proposed to introduce United Cigar Stores in that country, thereby revolutionizing the somewhat lackadaisical Gallic sales methods. In preparation for this they had established a school where they proposed to train a staff of bright young men who would be sent to France when the deal was consummated. Seemingly my experience with the American Tobacco Company gave me somewhat of an edge over the other applicants, as did the fact that I spoke French. In any case I got the job.

The negotiations with the French government dragged on and on and finally fell through completely. But in the meantime I had become an expert cigar-store manager, well versed in making plus sales and in withholding coupons from the customers whenever I legitimately could. I was also probably the only manager of a United Cigar Store who took time off to play in a country-club tennis tournament—this took only one day as I was put out in the first round without winning a single game—or who saw the Dempsey-Carpentier fight at Boyle's Thirty Acres in a box with Big Bill Edwards and two vice-presidents of the Guaranty Trust Company. But after all, wasn't I going to be an executive when I got to Paris, after the monopoly had been safely secured? And why, therefore, shouldn't I practice acting like one? It was no wonder, feeling as I did, that I resigned the very day it was finally announced that the French government had changed its mind. I definitely did not want to continue to meet the customer face to face across a glass counter. I had higher ambitions than that.

Unfortunately I still had no qualifications for any kind of a job. I had run through the financial world and the tobacco business with the speed of a Paddock, and nothing that I had learned in either of these fields was of the slightest assistance in getting a really good position. I made an abortive attempt to learn the department-store business from the ground up, the ground in this case being the storeroom of the drapery department. And I quit that job for a day to accept one as a sales clerk at Dunhill's new store, only to leave even before I started work and to dash back to Stern's for my storeroom job when I discovered I would have to wear a long linen duster as I waited on the customers at Dunhill's.

It was shortly after Stern's and I had parted company that I almost became a motion-picture producer. Away from parental supervision for the first time in my life a month or so after my twenty-first birthday, I had married a beautiful girl whom I had known for exactly seventy-two hours. And she happened to be the daughter of the founder and president of United Artists, the organization that released the films of Douglas Fairbanks and Mary Pickford and Charlie Chaplin and a few others among the giants of the screen of that day. Nepotism was then, as it is now, an important part of the picture business, and it was my new father-in-law's idea that I should at once be put in charge of a unit making a picture somewhere on Long Island. Naturally I agreed to this exciting suggestion, and everything was in the process of being worked out when a most unfortunate thing happened: my wife and I separated and in due course divorced. And with our divorce went my one and only chance of becoming a motion-picture producer.

And then my brother set up an appointment for me with Samuel Vauclain, the president of the Baldwin Locomotive Works in Philadelphia. With excited alacrity I took the job he offered me. Which is how I happened to become a boilermaker.

Actually, of course, I was not supposed to remain a boilermaker long. Ultimately, after I knew as much as I could possibly learn about the facts of making locomotives,

I was to become a locomotive salesman, and my territory was to be Russia, a natural assignment since I spoke that language well. But it would probably be at least three years, or so Vauclain estimated, before the Bolshevik government fell, and that would give me plenty of time to learn the business thoroughly. First I must learn how locomotives were made. And that meant that I would have to work at the Essington plant for a year, living as close to the plant as I could, since getting to work at seven in the morning, in the obligatory overalls, meant that I could not consider making the forty-minute trip from Philadelphia each day. I took a room in a boarding house a few minutes away from the plant and went to work.

I learned a great deal in the eight months I managed to stick it out at the Essington plant—but practically nothing of what I learned had to do with locomotives. I learned about the simple pleasures of simple men, and about the gusty, earthy humor of those who work with their hands. I learned about the cruelty of strength, and about the cold contempt of lusty men for the predatory women who prey on them. I learned about the almost divine power of foremen, and the sadism of company doctors. I learned about dirt, deep, penetrating grime and grit and grease, and I came to know the scraped feeling of a sandstoned body, red and tingling and somehow always dirty. I learned how to wash my hands in the inadequate facilities the shop provided for this purpose, so that I could eat my sandwich without tasting grease in every mouthful. I hated every minute of it—and as I grew older I realized increasingly that I would not have missed any of it for anything in the world.

But I didn't know it then, and there came a time when I felt I had to get out. I knew that I wasn't getting any place, and I was less and less certain of the accuracy of Vauclain's predictions about Russia. Unless he had some very secret information, and I was of the opinion he did not have access to any sources that could help him to implement his feelings in the matter, it did not seem very likely that the Bolshevik government was toppling. If anything it appeared to be getting stronger every day. And I saw no point in spending years in a business I had come to hate if my basic reasons for staying in it were never to be achieved. I quit my job and moved back to New York.

I went to work for my brother in his newest venture, the Message Exchange. It was just one of a long series of odd ideas he had had since he had been given a check for one hundred thousand dollars by the White Motor Company in appreciation of his work for them in Czarist Russia. These ventures had included an import and export firm to specialize in the South American market, started in partnership with and under the name of Hamilton Fish, my brother's classmate at Harvard. The collapse of the South American market brought this business to a speedy close. It was followed by a whole series of promotional ventures, including a new method of prolonging the life of railroad ties by treating them with creosote; the purchase of an island in the West Indies for the purpose of growing a very special kind of long-staple cotton—this particular venture had come to an end when a hurricane swept the island, leveling it completely and fouling all the water on the island with tons of salt water; and a number of other schemes, all of which failed to come to complete fruition.

When my brother died in 1935 he was in the midst of his most ambitious project. It was his idea to correct the stagnant condition of the automobile business in depression-struck America by shipping to Russia all the used cars cluttering the lots throughout the country. He planned to set up service centers all over that vast land and keep them supplied with parts for on-the-spot repairs. With the used cars all disposed of, he was certain that the automobile business in America would recover rapidly. Unfortunately he never got a chance to prove his point.

The Message Exchange too was an excellent idea, based on the sound premise that people catching trains, whether they were commuters or patrons of the Twentieth Century, always thought of last-minute messages they had no time to deliver. By stationing Green Caps at strategic points in the Grand Central and Pennsylvania stations my brother hoped to take care of these messages for them. For a small fee they could scribble out their words on convenient pads, and telephone calls would be made for them, or wires sent, or errands done, even while they were relaxing comfortably in the smoking car. There was only one thing wrong with the whole plan. The small fee could not possibly cover the costs of operation of the large organization that had to be maintained. On the other hand, a larger fee would have appreciably cut down the volume of business my brother hoped to obtain. He ran the Message Exchange at a heavy loss for a few years and then quit. But way before then I had finally found my career. In fact I found it while I was still working for him.

My duties with the Message Exchange had never been clearly defined. I did not wear a uniform or a green cap, nor could I have been called an executive. But one thing was very definite. I was absent from work every day for two hours, which time I spent on a couch in a darkened room in a very beautiful office on Park Avenue. I was soon well into my analysis.

In those days psychiatry was still a comparatively unknown science. There were only a few practitioners of it in the city, and they were all of them likely to be good men who were sincerely interested in exploring the possibilities of this new form of medicine. A few years later there were hundreds of them practicing, and a desire to be a psychoanalyst was almost all they had to have in order to set themselves up in business. But when I first went through the unforgettable experience of an analysis, I was, in a way, breaking new ground. This was doubly true in my case, since the man I went to was practicing in a new field, that of occupational therapy. As far as I know he was the real pioneer in it.

I went to him for six months. At the end of that time we sat facing each other in his office one day, the first time we had been in that position since my first visit to him. He tapped his pencil on the thick stack of notes he had taken on my case, and looked at me speculatively. "You should be a publisher," he said. He looked at me again and nodded. "Yes," he said, "that's what you should be. Have you ever thought of going into that field?"

I shook my head. I had to resist the impulse to ask him exactly what it was a publisher did. I admitted to him that it had never occurred to me to be one.

"Nevertheless," he said, "that is where you belong." Tapping his pencil, he looked at me again. "Do you know my friends the Knopfs?" he asked.

I nodded. "I've met them," I said. "Alfred Knopf's father was a good friend of my father's. And I've known Edwin for many years."

He came as close to smiling as I had known him to in all the time I'd been going to him. "Good," he said, reaching for the telephone on his desk. "I'll call them right away." He gave the operator the number and then turned to me. "You'll see," he said, "you'll see that I am right about this."

And that is how, after my short and variegated career in a half-dozen assorted businesses, I went to work in the field in which I have remained ever since. The good doctor was most definitely right. I shall always be grateful to him.

Of course it was inevitable that I should be expected to learn the publishing business from the ground up. I took this for granted. I had begun to think of myself as the eternal apprentice. Only this time even though I started my new life in the stock room at ten dollars a week, I enjoyed myself hugely. It was Knopf's idea that the most important basic fact was to become acquainted with the titles the firm was publishing and selling, and with the relative importance of the various book stores in the country. And there could be no question that you learned these things most quickly while you filled orders and packed them. I worked in the stock room for three months, and I've never forgotten the things I learned there. They were to come in handy for my entire publishing life.

There was another thing that made working at Knopf's exciting. The list appearing under the Borzoi imprint at that time was a truly magnificent one, and it gave me a solid grounding in contemporary literature. I filled orders for Thomas Mann's *Buddenbrooks* and Willa Cather's *A Lost Lady* and Thomas Beer's *Stephen Crane* and Floyd Dell's *Janet March* and Carl Van Vechten's *The Blind Bow-Boy*. And there were books by Katherine Mansfield and G. B. Stern, Arthur Machen and M. P. Shiel, E. M. Forster, A. E. Coppard, Ivan Bunin, T. F. Powys, Conrad Aiken, Walter de la Mare, Max Beerbohm, Joseph Hergesheimer, Hilaire Belloc, Julian Huxley—and Marie, Queen of Roumania. There were also three books that, although we naturally did not know it then, foreshadowed the whole of the next quarter century, *Fascism*, *The World-Struggle for Oil*, and *The Atom and the Bohr Theory of its Structure*. I read them all avidly, every book on the shelves. I was beginning to discover what the psychiatrist had meant. I was discovering a new world.

And yet I have always had a sneaking suspicion that the fact Knopf was planning to move from his offices on West

Forty-second Street to new and very elaborate quarters in the Heckscher Building had something to do with my being taken on by him. Of course it might have been pure coincidence that two other apprentices came to work for him shortly after I started, both of them in the stock room too. And when the move was made less than six weeks later, the whole staff, the three apprentices included, worked day and night for almost two weeks, packing everything in the old offices, helping the movers move, and then putting things together in the new location.

The other two apprentices left shortly after the move uptown had been made. I stayed on, but not in the stock room. I was given a sort of roving job in the accounting department, and when that did not seem to be the proper place for me, I was transferred to the *American Mercury*. There I had the job of trying to get advertising for that excellent magazine, but it was an almost hopeless assignment at the time. Less than four issues had been published, no definite circulation figures could be guaranteed, the general opinion was that the high literary quality of the magazine did not make it an ideal medium for general advertising—and I was a completely inept space salesman. I am sure that there was not too much unhappiness in the Knopf offices when I offered my resignation.

But it was only from Knopf that I was resigning. I had fallen in love with the publishing business, and I proposed to stay in it. I had been approached by Boni & Liveright, and it was there I was going.

TWO

―――――――――――――――――――

BOY
PUBLISHER

*I*T's Manuel Komroff's favorite story. I have heard him tell it many times, leaning against a convenient fireplace, his drooping mustaches making him look like a fugitive from *Taras Bulba*.

"Donald was my assistant in the manufacturing department of Boni & Liveright," he will say, with that strange laugh of his, which in anybody else would be called a titter. "So when I wanted something done that morning I naturally asked Donald to do it." He really laughs then, shaking quietly for a full minute. "And do you know what he said to me?" he asks. "He looked at me calmly and said 'I'm sorry, Man. You'll have to get somebody else to do that for you. You see, I'm vice-president of the company now.'"

Actually Komroff exaggerates only very slightly. I was twenty-four years old in the summer of 1925 when Horace Liveright sold me a half interest in the company and gave me the title of "First Vice-President"—the "First" was very important since already there were three vice-presidents in the firm. At that time the sum total of my experience in publishing consisted of the six months I had spent with Alfred Knopf and a year with Liveright.

Komroff tells a story about our interview when I left Knopf and went to work for Boni & Liveright, which pleases him only slightly less than the other one. He continues to claim that he hired me on the basis that there must be something good in somebody who has been fired from three colleges: Harvard, Yale, and Princeton. Since nobody has ever been able to explain the qualities that make for a desirable publisher's employee, I suppose that his deduction was sound enough. Certainly I have every reason to be grateful to Komroff. Through him I got a ringside seat at a show that has never been equaled, and probably never will be: the literary explosion of the 1920's.

And Boni & Liveright was just about the best place I could have chosen as an observation point. For one thing, all the accepted ideas about publishing had been thrown out the window, and every book was a new challenge to the ingenuity of the oddly assorted staff. Everything, in their opinion, was worth trying at least once. And the results were spectacular in the extreme.

There was, for instance, the building itself, a four-story brownstone on West Forty-eighth Street, in deliberate defiance of the publishing axiom that dignity and dust were the mark of the successful publisher. There was certainly no dignity here. Converted from a conservative dwelling to the purposes it now served, the building was a rambling hive, from the shipping room in the basement to the hot little rooms on the top floor where the advertising department laid out the splash campaigns for which the firm was famous—campaigns as often as not planned without consulting with the manufacturing or sales departments, with disastrous results. On the floors between were the executive offices, looking as much as possible like comfortable living-rooms, with not a single conventional desk in evidence. There were also Liveright's private shower and the comfortable parlor, with its grand piano, which

17

served as a reception and waiting-room. Leading off it was a canopied terrace, well equipped with lounge chairs, which in the hot summer months was a favorite resting place for hot and thirsty authors. Later when Liveright branched out into play production something else was added. An opening was cut through into the adjoining building, and a door in the form of a fake bookcase was installed. It was for us a never-ending source of amusement to watch the expressions on the faces of the people in the waiting-room when the bookcase would suddenly swing into the room and a startlingly beautiful secretary would glide out to summon an equally beautiful actress to her interview in the theatrical offices.

The staff itself was extraordinary. Dick Simon had left a short time before I came in, and was already well started on his meteoric publishing career. But Bennett Cerf was still there, as blandly disarming then as he is today, and fully as joke-conscious. His last legacy to the firm, before he persuaded Liveright to sell him the Modern Library for what turned out to be a song, was Anita Loos's *Gentlemen Prefer Blondes*, which he alone of everybody in the firm felt could be a run-away best seller. Ralph Barton did the hilarious illustrations for the book, and it was arbitrarily priced at two dollars in the first catalog announcements. But in a sales conference it was decided, without discussing the matter with the manufacturing department, that that was too much to charge for a humorous book, and the price was reduced to a dollar seventy-five. It wasn't until sometime later, after the book had sold well into the hundred thousands, that it was discovered that the manufacturing cost of the book was so high that we were losing money on every copy we sold. The price was hastily increased to two dollars, but the major sales had already been made by then, and we never did recoup our losses.

There was another galling point in connection with this

book. Every publishing contract calls for the payment of half royalties on sales to Canada, in order to provide for increased discounts to Canadian accounts to cover import duties. This clause had unfortunately been left out of the contract on this book, as we discovered to our sorrow when Anita Loos and her husband John Emerson came to see us after they had received their first royalty check. They were very sorry about the whole thing. They understood fully that contracts usually provided for reduced royalties on Canadian sales. But as they pointed out to us with incontrovertible logic, the contract on *Gentlemen Prefer Blondes* did not so provide, and would we please pay Miss Loos the full royalties on the not inconsiderable Canadian sales? We paid.

It was right after Cerf had bought the Modern Library and had set up shop for himself that Liveright offered me a partnership in the firm. My mother insists that Cerf wanted me to join him in purchasing the Modern Library and advised against my making a financial investment in Boni & Liveright. But that is not my recollection of what happened. In any case I thought the whole Modern Library venture sounded entirely too commercial to appeal to me. It was one thing to operate the Modern Library as part of a general publishing house, but to devote oneself completely to it was to become nothing more than a reprint publisher, a merchandiser of proven wares. If I ever did have this opportunity, and I repeat that I cannot remember the discussions with Cerf that my mother has often quoted to me since then, I am sure I never gave it serious thought. As for Random House, the well-fed dog that now wags the fat Modern Library tail, it was at that time, to the best of my knowledge, not even a gleam in Cerf's eye. Even when it was first thought of in connection with the publication of a limited edition of *Candide* with illustrations by Rockwell Kent, it was intended to cover exactly what the name implied: occasional publications by a ghostly animal activated by that very healthy tail, the Modern Library.

In any case I leaped at the chance Liveright offered me. I had been left a good deal of money by my father, although the amount would have been much greater if the Russian Revolution had not come along just when it did. As the Ford agent for all of Russia, and later as the leading representative for the majority of American automobiles in that country as well, Father had done extremely well. But a great part of his holdings were in branch offices and merchandise throughout that vast country, and while he anticipated the revolt that finally came, there was no way he could liquidate these assets, and they, as well as a good part of his deposits in various Russian banks, were wiped out overnight when the Bolsheviks took over. Nevertheless he had managed to make some rather substantial transfers to American banks, and it was part of my share of these monies that I now proposed to invest in Boni & Liveright.

It was not, however, quite as simple as all that. There were complications. My father had died when I was only a few months past my twentieth birthday, and seemingly suspecting the fact that I might not prove to be as good a businessman as he had been, he had left my share of his estate in trust for me. My older brother and my mother were the administrators of this trust fund, and I was permitted to draw liberally on the income from the excellent investments my father had made. But drawing on capital was something else again. That called for careful consideration and for expensive auditors and for even more expensive lawyers. And the auditors shook their heads in bewilderment as publishing practice was explained to them, and the lawyers recoiled in horror at the casual way publishers conducted their business. And I argued and I pleaded and I tried to explain things I myself understood only vaguely. At times it was difficult to decide whether I was the buyer or the seller. But finally I succeeded in getting the consent of my mother and brother. Grudgingly they permitted me to use a hundred and ten thousand dollars of my inheritance to buy a half interest in Boni & Liveright.

The actual contract negotiations had their humorous aspect too. I had come down with a serious sinus attack and had moved from my apartment to the Harbor Hospital, a private clinic on the upper floors of a building on Madison Avenue and Sixty-second Street. It was a very pleasant hospital, and since I felt perfectly well most of the time except when I was suffering from an actual attack, I enjoyed myself hugely. This was particularly true in view of the fact that the ground floor of the building was occupied by the Colony Restaurant, then as now among the greatest in the world. I saw the lawyers in my hospital room, and I entertained in it with what seemed to be an endless stream of waiters from downstairs bringing food and drink for my guests and me. Under these almost ideal circumstances the contract was finally signed, and I emerged from the hospital several pounds heavier and a full partner in the most flamboyant publishing house of all time. As I have said before, I was then just twenty-four years old, having celebrated my birthday in the hospital.

Even with Cerf gone the personnel of Boni & Liveright was unusually exciting. Manuel Komroff's first book of short stories had not yet appeared, and he was just finishing work on his edition of Marco Polo, which was to be the first volume in that exciting series of books called the Black and Gold Library. In the meantime he presided benignly over the manufacturing department, experimenting with new papers and cloths for bindings and producing books that, when he was permitted to do as he wanted, were inferior only to the really remarkable books Knopf was issuing. All the other publishers seemed to feel that to try for beauty in trade books was somehow rather effete, a feeling shared a good part of the time by those in our firm who had the harrowing duty of seeing that the bills got paid.

T. R. Smith was editor-in-chief. Cherubic and acidulous, and a remarkable drinker, he gave the impression that he considered associating with most of our authors a form of slumming. He was probably one of the most erudite editors any publishing house has ever had. He was also a great scholar in the fields of erotica, and some of the finest books in that category were published by him under various fictitious imprints, with illustrations by Clara Tice and others. He was the only editor with whom George Moore would work, and except for periods of varying duration when they refused to speak to each other, the only editor Theodore Dreiser would permit to touch his manuscripts. In the summer of 1925 they were definitely not speaking: it had been T. R.'s unenviable duty to cut *An American Tragedy* some hundred thousand words.

Assisting him were George Kaufman's wife Beatrice and later a very bright young man named Louis Kronenberger. Their approach to a problem was diametrically opposite, which made for a balanced evaluation. The sales manager of the company was Julian Messner, who later also founded his own firm. And one of the junior assistants in the advertising department was a young girl, Lillian Hellman, who had taken this as her first job.

And looming above all of us, and over the others who came and went as people are inclined to do in any profession, there was Horace Liveright himself.

He was a thin man, thin almost to the point of emaciation, and probably the most nervous one I have ever known. His gaunt face was topped with a shock of black hair, and he could have played the part of Mephistopheles without the slightest trace of make-up. He was utterly ruthless and completely self-centered. He was also a magnificent host and an irresistible force as far as women were concerned. The same was true of men. In fact he drew anybody he wanted into the orbit of his charm without the slightest difficulty. And since he could never bear the thought of being alone he kept himself surrounded with people at all times, beautiful women and brilliant men alike, in a complete surrender to a form of compulsive gregariousness.

Not that he particularly liked the people who flocked about him. He hated most of them and was fully aware of the fact that they would turn on him at the slightest indication of a lessening of his power. Probably this feeling was nurtured by the knowledge that there was within his own organization a carefully planned conspiracy to take advantage of his financial weakness and to reduce him to the position of an impotent figurehead. It involved only a very few of his associates, but they happened to be key figures, occupying positions that made it possible for them to function with the greatest possible effectiveness. And yet he could do nothing about it except hope that he could always keep one step ahead of them. This was undoubtedly the reason for most of his flamboyant gestures. He had to risk his all on every roll of the dice in order to head off those who had set out to destroy him.

His personal financial situation was always precarious. He was heavily involved in the stock market, and his tipsters were no more reliable than most tipsters usually are, even if he did include among them such figures as his particular friend Otto Kahn. The trouble was that Kahn was on the inside and Liveright was not, and the difference between profit and loss on their involved operations lay in the almost split-second decisions that had to be made and acted upon without the slightest delay. Kahn could do this. It was, after all, his whole business life. But Liveright would necessarily always be a little behind him, and that was usually fatal. Even in the lush days of the bull market he managed to lose money on his stock-exchange transactions. And when the crash came he was wiped out to the last penny. It was a bitter shock to him, made more so by the fact that when it finally and inevitably happened all of his holdings in his own firm were in the hands of the money lenders who had advanced him large sums against his shares—at almost usurious rates.

Liveright and I were never particularly friendly. There was no real bond between us, no actual point of contact. I tried not to remind myself of the fact that I was a partner in the firm only because I had happened to have some money Liveright needed badly for his own personal reasons. I found it very difficult to forget this. Not that he ever threw it in my face or even intimated that he too was aware of it. Actually he managed to lean over backward in living up to his share of the bargain. But I knew that I did not have the qualifications to hold up my end, and I was very conscious of the lip service paid me by the older and more experienced people in the office who suddenly found themselves relegated to positions inferior to mine. I do not blame them for feeling as they did. I would probably have the same feelings myself if a twenty-four-year-old boy suddenly came into a firm I had helped develop, and was put in the position of telling me what I should do.

We went to each other's parties. We consulted each other meticulously. We discussed our differences of opinion frankly and with no punches pulled. And yet we were never, and in no way, really partners. One reason for this was, of course, that Liveright was head and shoulders above all of us, and particularly above me, as an inspired publisher. He knew this to be true and he didn't care who knew that he knew it. It was in one unforgettable flashing moment late in our relationship, only a few months, as a matter of fact, before we parted company, that I came to realize this fact fully and finally.

I had come to his office to discuss something with him, and we had sat together for a full half-hour, talking, laughing, planning whatever it was that we had to plan. We were laughing when I got to the door of his office, and I turned to open it. And then I remembered something I had forgotten to say, and turned back suddenly into the room. I can still feel the shock I experienced when I looked at him. A moment before he had been smiling, a warm smile that lit up the aquiline face with its piercing eyes. Now, barely a second or two later, there was no trace of it. His face was cold and it was cruel—colder and crueler than any I have ever seen. I had caught him off guard, and it was probably the first time it had ever happened to him. The smile came back instantaneously, the eyes shone warmly once more, the face became mobile. But I could never again look at him without thinking about that moment and about his mastery of the removable smile.

Actually I suppose that was the key to his character. He was a man born to be unhappy, born to be ridden by ambition and a will for power. He drove himself mercilessly, using every ounce of his enormous energy, until he had exhausted himself and had to rely more and more on stimulants to keep himself going. He was as much the pyramiding speculator as a publisher as any stock-market operator who kept piling paper profits on paper profits. Tomorrow would be bonanza day. So why not spend today? The trouble with this reasoning was that it was impossible to show a profit on publishing operations in view of the fantastic sums that were spent on advertising. And without this advertising sales would have been cut in half or more. I was peculiarly aware of this problem. There was in the treasurer's office a card available only to him, Liveright, and me. It was a daily record of cash in the bank, accounts payable, accounts receivable, and so forth. And it at all times showed a bank balance five thousand dollars smaller than was actually the case. Liveright never knew about this. We saw to that. If he had known there was that much more money in the bank, it would have been spent —for another overgenerous advance or for additional advertising on some book that did not seem to be reacting as it should to the already large sums that had been spent on it.

There was something else about Liveright that made him almost unique in the publishing world. He rarely, if ever, read a book or a manuscript. And yet his list was during the top years of the firm the most phenomenal list ever assembled by any publisher. And Liveright was responsible for the greater part of it. He seemed to have the ability to smell out good books, a second sense about them, as if he could tell by looking at one whether or not it was worth publishing. Certainly he had that second sense about writers. He was an almost inspired evaluator of people, and his list was built around his personal judgment of their possibilities. If he believed in an author no advance was too liberal and no advertising schedule too lavish. And he was right most of the time. The trouble was that when he was wrong he was no less spectacularly wrong. And that made it very hard to maintain an equitable balance between profits and losses.

And yet it is hard to see how Boni & Liveright could help but make money. Take the 1925 fall list for example, probably the most incredible list ever issued by any publishing house. The leaders in fiction were Dreiser's *An American Tragedy* and Sherwood Anderson's *Dark Laughter*. There was also a new novel by Gertrude Atherton, *The Crystal Cup*, her first novel since *Black Oxen*. There were novels by Heywood Broun and Paul Morand and Naomi Royde-Smith and Konrad Bercovici, all potential big sellers. There were *Gentlemen Prefer Blondes* and the first publication in America of Roger Martin du Gard's

The Thibaults, which later won for him the Nobel Prize. And there was a volume of short stories called *In Our Time*, which was to mark the debut of a young writer named Ernest Hemingway. It preceded by only a few months our publishing of the first book by another young writer, William Faulkner.

In non-fiction too were some choice titles. There were new books by Van Loon and Ludwig Lewisohn and Sven Hedin, *The Medical Follies* by Morris Fishbein, and *The Revolt of Modern Youth* by Judge Ben Lindsey. There was a luxurious limited edition of the *Droll Stories*, illustrated by Ralph Barton, and the first volumes of the Scott Moncrieff translation of Stendhal. There were new editions of George Moore and of Eugene O'Neill, of Lewis Mumford and Harry Kemp, of Anna Louise Strong and Sigmund Freud, of Sigmund Spaeth and John D. Rockefeller Jr., of T. S. Eliot and Edgar Lee Masters and Ezra Pound. And there was an unusually thick volume of poetry, *Roan Stallion, Tamar and Other Poems*, which was Robinson Jeffers's first major publication.

It is hard to imagine any publisher being able to lose money on such a list. And yet I have before me the auditor's statement for the year of 1925. It shows sales of just under one million dollars—and a net profit of exactly $8,609.12.

Actually nobody cared very much. Certainly I didn't. It was much too exciting to interview a bearded and bashful writer with a first novel that Sherwood Anderson had suggested he submit to us, and to read *Soldier's Pay*, still to my mind as good as anything William Faulkner has ever written. It was much too exciting to send a cable to Paris offering publication to Hemingway on the strength of having read a privately published and very slim volume of short stories, and even more exciting to find out later that this unconventional method of approach had made it possible for us to secure his first book, since Maxwell Perkins of Scribner's, who also wanted to publish him, had written him a letter instead. And later when Liveright had turned down Hemingway's next book against our advice and instructions, and Hemingway had gone around the corner to Scribner's where a contract, arranged for in anticipation of just such a move by Scott Fitzgerald, was waiting for him, it was exciting to sit at a café table in the Place de l'Odéon with Hemingway, explaining to him what had happened, and having him say that some day he'd make it up to me. It was a lasting excitement too, since it was thirteen years before the opportunity arose for Hemingway to live up to his promise. I was a literary agent in Hollywood by then, and I flew up to Sun Valley to see him, to ask if I could handle the motion-picture sale of *For Whom the Bell Tolls*. I hadn't read the book yet, and the first thing that Hemingway did when I arrived at seven in the morning was to hand me a copy of it and suggest that I read it before we talked any further. And so I sat in my room for the next eight hours, completely immersed in this masterly novel, interrupted in my reading now and then by Hemingway or Martha Gellhorn or one of Hemingway's boys with a glass of wine and a sandwich and an eager "How do you like it?" I barely managed to finish the book at that. I am afraid that I read the last hundred or so pages in an alcoholic haze. But the result of that day in Sun Valley was my very first sale as an agent, and at the then phenomenal price of one hundred and fifty thousand dollars, fifty thousand dollars more than had ever been paid for the film rights to a book.

And that was just part of the picture. It was exciting to arrange a dinner for Dreiser and Anderson and O'Neill, the three literary giants of the day, who somehow had never spent an evening together: Dreiser, massive and insatiably curious, his handkerchief carefully folded and refolded while he talked in that characteristic gesture of his, asking questions of O'Neill as respectfully as any aspiring young dramatist in Professor Baker's classes; O'Neill, solemn and humorless, almost unearthly in his asceticism, letting the words flow out of him as if they had hardly any connection with him; and all the while Anderson, looking like a well-fed business man who had suddenly decided to wear an artist's flowing tie, trying to amuse them, telling stories, asking questions, reveling in the unusual opportunity that was his. The sequel, as far as Anderson was concerned, was typical. A few months after the dinner there appeared in *Vanity Fair* a story by Anderson. It began: "I once told a ghost-story to Theodore Dreiser and Eugene O'Neill."

There were other things too that made the fact we were just breaking even at best seem singularly unimportant. There was the time a very quiet man, with an accent that made it hard to understand him, was permitted to sit for almost the entire day in the lower waiting-room. True, he had asked to see Liveright; but then many people wanted to see him, and he was a busy man. And the name the receptionist had given to Liveright's secretary rang no bell with her. So he sat patiently, waiting, wondering, no doubt, about these strange Americans. It was late in the afternoon when T. R., unable to control his curiosity any longer, went up to him and discovered to his amazement that the quiet little man was Sven Hedin, just in from Sweden with his new manuscript, *My Life as an Explorer*.

Actually such things did not happen very often. As the junior member of the firm, I had the job of seeing the casuals who came in to our offices. Therefore I also drew all the crackpots and nuts. There were at least three Jesus Christs among them, including one very odoriferous one who assembled what he called his manuscript from bits of paper, covered with illegible scrawls, which he kept pulling out of all his coat and vest and trouser pockets. And there was a strange looking woman who tried to interest me in a manuscript she had written about love cults. She was, she assured me, an expert on the subject. After all, her younger sister was at that very moment a member of one. And when I still assured her that we would not be interested in such a book, she tried a new tack. She was a fortune teller too, she informed me. Would I like my fortune told? Politely I asked her what she read, cards or the palm or the bumps on the head. Nothing as simple as that, she said. She had invented an absolutely new and completely infallible system. Maybe that would make a book, she suggested. As a matter of fact, she continued, it might make a very interesting book. "You see," she said, "I read the phallus."

The editorial meetings were exciting too. There was a peculiar arrangement between Liveright and me whereby we could each of us accept books that the editorial committee had rejected, provided we guaranteed the firm against losses. Some very strange works got on his list in this manner. There was a collection of speeches by Liveright's good friend and theatrical angel Otto Kahn, a book on education by the completely unknown headmaster of the school in which Liveright's son was a pupil, and a slim volume of poetry by the son of a leading movie magnate. My own list seems even stranger as I look at it now. It included a book on Caruso's voice methods by a cousin of mine, a novel by an English writer which seemingly appealed to me because the central character was named Donald, a book on glands by Louis Berman, and a series of books by Krishnamurti. It also included a projected book on reading fortunes in coffee grounds, which was a joint project of Romany Marie and Harry Kemp, and was to be illustrated by Brancusi, and a reprint, from the Nonesuch Press edition, of *Irene Iddesleigh* by Mrs. Amanda M'Kittrick Ros. Here is a sample from it. "Speak! Irene! Wife!

Woman! Do not sit in silence and allow the blood that now
boils in my veins to ooze through cavities of unrestrained
passion and trickle down to drench me with its crimson
hue!" As I remember it I was particularly proud of getting
this book on the list. As I also remember, it set a new low
record for sales that was never approached by any other
book on our list.

One other of these "personal" books had a ridiculously
funny aftermath. I put a novel by Thomas Mann's son
Klaus, *The Fifth Child*, on our list, and I thought it would
help the book if I could arrange an American lecture tour
for Klaus and his twin sister Erika. The lecture business
was booming then, as was everything else, and I had no
trouble in selling the idea to one of our leading lecture
bureaus and in getting them to put up money for steamship passage for the Manns. A fine schedule was arranged,
and it looked as if my plan was going to prove a brilliant
one. Only a single detail had been overlooked, and when I
met Klaus and Erika at the dock it was obviously too late
to remedy this oversight on our part: we had neglected to
ask them if they spoke English, and it turned out that they
did not.

But these books were the exception rather than the rule.
Usually there was complete editorial agreement. And why
shouldn't there be? For in addition to our powerhouse of
a list of writers we kept adding exciting new ones each
season: Dorothy Parker, Samuel Hoffenstein, Bertrand
Russell's *Education and the Good Life*, Jacob Wassermann,
Hermann Sudermann, W. E. Woodward and his "debunk-
ing" biography of George Washington, the plays of George
S. Kaufman and John Colton and Stark Young and Philip
Barry, Wolfgang Kohler's *Gestalt Psychology*, Frances
Newman's extraordinary books, Isadora Duncan's *My Life*,
and Francis Hackett's *Henry the Eighth*.

This last book was always good for fifteen minutes of

serious debate. Hackett took four years longer to write it than he had planned to take, and there were constant requests for additional advances to enable him to finish it. In the negative was our treasurer, who kept pleading for us to take our loss and be done with it. In the affirmative was Liveright, confident that the book was a certain success, so what did another two thousand in advances matter? And backing him up was T. R. Smith, the same T. R. who once advised us very casually to pay two thousand dollars outright for all English-speaking rights to a biography that had just been published in Germany. "No book on Napoleon," he assured us, "has ever sold less than four thousand copies in the two countries." The book was of course Emil Ludwig's *Napoleon*. After over two hundred thousand copies of it had been sold in America alone, it was decided that we should no longer stick to the letter of the contract. From then on, Ludwig was informed, he would receive royalties on all copies sold.

There were other moments too: the time Frances Newman sent us a fuschia blossom with orders to match it exactly for the binding of her book *The Hard-Boiled Virgin*; the time we lost the manuscript of Warner Fabian's new novel, *Summer Bachelors*, and Samuel Hopkins Adams who had made no copy of it had to rewrite the entire book from memory; the time I went to see Isadora Duncan in her studio in Paris, a few months before her death, to try to persuade her to finish her book, and she lay, fat and blowzy and half drunk, on the tattered couch in the corner of the room describing with wide and unbelievably graceful movements of her arms the dance Irma Duncan had taught her pupils as a greeting to her on her trip to Russia, all this against an obbligato of interruptions by a continuous stream of creditors whom I had to satisfy then and there; the time Djuna Barnes and I sat in her attic in Paris going over her new book and substituting asterisks for every letter of every word we felt would have to be cut out of the book if it were to get by the censors; the time I took the ethereal Elinor Wylie, who lived her life out in the firm belief that she was Shelley reborn, to a chili joint on lower Sixth Avenue and watched her eat two bowls of chili so hot that the first bite I took paralyzed my taste buds for twenty-four hours; the time we met for tea in the Continental Hotel in Paris, and I asked George Moore, who happened to come in just then, to join us, only to regret it a moment later when Elinor left the table in tears after George Moore had stated flatly that there was no such thing as a woman novelist; the time I went to pay my respects to Moore in London just before sailing for America, and was greeted at the door by the seventy-one-year-old writer in slippers and dressing gown, who informed me that he could not possibly see me then as he was expecting a young lady any minute.

Who, with all this going on about him, could bother about making money? Publishing was for fun, and so was the publisher's life. There were other ways to get rich. There was the infallible stock market, which kept going up and up and up. There were first-edition collecting and the better than gilt-edge security of mint copies of Millay and Hemingway and Milne. And there was always the exciting speculation of producing plays.

░░░░░░░░░░░░░░░░░░░░░░░

ANGEL

WITH

CLIPPED

WINGS

To THE best of my knowledge Pascal Covici, with whom I later founded Covici, Friede, was never involved in play production. That was probably fortunate for him, because I shall never forget his reaction to one play he had been invited to see in dress rehearsal. After the final curtain he went backstage and argued with the dramatist and the novelist on whose book the play was based in a vain effort to persuade them to close the show then and there. He told them, and he said the same things to me the following morning, that it didn't have a chance, that it was going to be a complete failure, that it should be withdrawn before the critics and the public had a chance to see the horror that had been devised. Fortunately for them they did not follow his advice. The play happened to be *Tobacco Road*.

Horace Liveright, on the other hand, was definitely stage-struck. In fact there was a period in his career when he was much more interested in the theater than in publishing. And this period happened to coincide with my association with him. Naturally I was not immune to the fever.

His first independent production was already in the casting stage when I became a partner in Boni & Liveright in 1925. It was *Hamlet in Modern Clothes*, an American version of a project that had had a very successful run in England. It seemed like a good idea. It would graphically demonstrate the timelessness of Shakespeare, and it would be much less expensive to mount than the usual production. He had managed to get Basil Sydney for the lead, Helen Chandler for his Ophelia, and Ernest Lawford for the part of Polonius.

I was offered a chance to invest twenty-five hundred dollars in the production, and I leaped at it. It seemed incredibly exciting to me. To be able to go backstage at will, to sit in empty theaters watching rehearsals, to go to the first night feeling that I had had a part in bringing all those people in the audience into the theater—I wouldn't have missed it for the world. And besides, it was such a good investment. The production cost was low, and so was the running cost. With only a moderate success I could not help but recoup my investment. And if it was a smash hit, and we did not see how it could help but be, then I stood to make a great deal of money indeed. I was very grateful to Liveright for asking me to come in with him.

Of course things did not work out quite as we had expected. In fact they did not work out at all. The critics were only lukewarm about the whole idea. The public was definitely not interested; seemingly they took the attitude that if they saw *Hamlet* they wanted not only the Dane himself but also all the accepted trappings. After a two-week run to increasingly emptier houses we all stepped out and handed the production over to the actors. They ran it on a co-operative basis for a few more weeks at a theater far uptown on Fifth Avenue. Then they too gave up. Even lavishly distributed free tickets could not fill the small house in which they were playing.

But I had been bitten by the bug, and I told myself that the only thing wrong with my first venture was that I should never have gone into it at all. Obviously nobody wanted to see *Hamlet* in modern clothes. In fact very few people wanted to see *Hamlet* in any form. I should have realized that. We all should have. Now a musical or a play without the schoolroom flavor of *Hamlet*—that was different. People just did not want to see Shakespeare.

My next bout with the theater came in the following year. It was in connection with a musical called *Bad Habits of 1926*, which opened and closed almost simultaneously at the Greenwich Village Theater. The theater itself was torn down a short while later, but I do not think there was any connection between the two events.

In any case I got involved in this project in a very curious way. I had a good friend named Arthur Herzog who was desperately trying to convince his family that he was a born composer and lyricist. Since he had as yet been unable to get any of his songs published, he was having some difficulty in making his point with them. He in turn had a friend, Manning Sherwin, who was faced with the identical problem. It made for a bond between them, and they were soon working night and day together in an attempt to effect jointly what neither of them seemed able to do alone.

I had another good friend, a girl with the incredible name of Hume Derr. And she was very much in love with a struggling young would-be actor, John Lee Mahin. And one of his closest friends was another young actor who somehow seemed unable to get any parts on Broadway, a good-looking boy named Robert Montgomery.

We kept open house on Sundays, and this little group of

people could always be counted on to be there, playing dominoes or bagatelle, or standing around the piano singing. And out of these meetings grew the idea for a review to be written by Herzog, with music by Sherwin, and with Hume Derr, Robert Montgomery, and John Lee Mahin heading the small cast. There was to be one skit we were certain would assure the play of success. It was set at the seaside, and the entire cast was to play it in bathing suits. The musical number it was to feature was a life-guard's song entitled *I'm a Son of the Beach*, and we were convinced that it would wow any audience as completely as it did us.

A producer was found who felt that the whole idea had merit, and rehearsals began. Just as often as not they took place in our apartment, with occasional interruptions, as for instance when Hume and John Mahin suddenly decided to elope to Greenwich and get married, taking most of the cast with them as witnesses. But somehow things managed to take shape, and the night of the opening approached. It was then that I really became involved in a major way.

I had become connected with the project as much because of the fact that I wanted to prove to Liveright that I too could put on plays as for any other reason. Besides, the required investment was small, and we were convinced that the sheet sale of the music alone would bring us back many times the amount it would take to put on the review. But inevitably the expenses increased, and the day before the opening every last penny had been spent, and the matter of an Equity bond had still not been taken care of. Naturally it was to me that they all turned, and naturally I posted the necessary money so that the show could go on. And naturally I never saw any of it again.

The opening night was an experience in embarrassment that I am sure all of us wanted to forget as quickly as possible. I doubt if any revue has ever been so harshly panned by the critics, or what was even worse, so completely ignored by the public. It cured Mahin of the acting bug, and he went on to become one of the really great motion-picture writers. It didn't do Robert Montgomery much harm because so few people ever saw it. It did not discourage Manning Sherwin, who many years later was to write one of the top songs of the second World War, *A Nightingale Sang in Berkeley Square*. And somehow it did not discourage me either. It merely made me add musicals to Shakespeare as something I should stay clear of in the future.

In the meantime Liveright was preparing two plays for fall 1926 production. One was Patrick Kearney's dramatization of *An American Tragedy*, and the other was a play about a Negro prize fighter by Jim Tully and Frank Dazey, for which they finally settled on the title of *Black Boy*. I was offered a chance to invest in both plays, but I had just taken my loss on *Bad Habits* and did not have enough extra money to take advantage of Liveright's offer in full. Besides, *An American Tragedy* was to be a very expensive production, and an investment in it of some twenty-five hundred dollars would only get me a very small share. There was also the important fact to be considered that as Dreiser's publisher I shared in any motion-picture money in any case. I chose *Black Boy* as my next venture, not only for these reasons, but also because it was to be produced for a comparatively small amount, thereby increasing my chances of recouping my previous losses.

From the very beginning it was an exciting experience. Liveright had bought the play as a starring vehicle for Paul Robeson, even then nationally recognized as an outstanding figure in the world of the theater. It was obvious that his huge athlete's body would strip well on the stage, and his resonant and beautiful voice could not help but add meaning to his lines. We were very proud of ourselves when we signed the contract with him one morning at the office, and Liveright suggested that Robeson and his wife Essie meet us there at noon: we would all go out to lunch and celebrate the event.

When they had left I turned to Liveright. Where, I asked, did he plan to go for lunch? Any place, he answered —probably our favorite speakeasy down the street, where we usually lunched. Well, I said, didn't he think it might be a good idea to telephone and find out how they would feel about our bringing the Robesons? Nonsense, Liveright said. They would be proud to serve him.

But I persisted. And I was glad I had; not only did that speakeasy inform us that they would be unable to serve us if we came with the Robesons, but we got the same answer from every restaurant and speakeasy we called. Even the Algonquin asked us if we would mind eating in a private dining-room they would be happy to put at our disposal. Liveright was shaking with rage. But the lunch problem still had not been solved, and the Robesons would be back any minute now. I finally called my home and arranged for us to lunch there. And then I suddenly had another thought. The telephone calls and the rebuffs with which we had met had made me furious. They had also made me doubt everybody. What if our colored cook should object to serving the Robesons? That would be the final calamity. I called her and put the question to her point-blank. She laughed aloud at my doubts and assured me that nothing would make her feel prouder. And she magically turned out a magnificent lunch on less than an hour's notice.

We came up against the color problem again and again. At least three of the top actresses in America were anxious and willing to play the female lead opposite Robeson. It was a rich part, that of an unwitting Delilah, and it called for really good acting. And yet it soon became obvious that it would be tempting fate to cast a white woman in the part. It would have angered the critics, or so we came to feel, and it would have antagonized the theater-going public and kept them away in droves. Finally an excellent colored actress was found for the part. She was obviously not as good as the stars we could have had if it had not been for the strange situation with which we were faced, but we felt we had no choice in the matter.

Even the question of out-of-town try-outs came to be tied in with the fact that Robeson was colored. The play finally was tried out in Mamaroneck, more for the reason that I had a large summer home in near-by Larchmont, which did away with the hotel problem, than for any other reason. And even then I had to shut my eyes to what our ultra-conservative neighbors would think about our house guests.

One of the big moments in the play was an offstage fight in which Black Boy loses the major bout of his career. The broadcasting of prize fights had still not become a Gillette Razor monopoly, and the only expert in the field was the man who had pioneered it himself, Major J. Andrew White. I knew him quite well from the fact that he was associated with the first radio store of the period, Haynes-Griffin, and I suggested that he be employed to broadcast the fictitious fight, which Black Boy's girl was supposed to hear over the radio in their apartment. It proved to be a good suggestion, even though it turned out to involve the inventing of practically an entirely new public-address system. The major rewrote his script to conform to his ideas of how a fight should sound when it is broadcast. He did a good job of it too. We lived in constant fear though that something would go wrong with his equipment. If it had, we would really have been in trouble: expert radio repair men were not at that time a dime a dozen.

But there were no real mishaps in connection with the production. The director was excellent, Robeson was marvelous, the supporting cast more than adequate. Even Liveright's almost disastrous attempt to cut costs by eliminating all lighting rehearsals did no permanent harm. The only trouble was that the leading woman was just not good enough for the part. It was a fact that became increasingly obvious as the night of the Broadway opening drew nearer. And there was nothing we could do about it. Owing to the practically nonexistent demand for experienced colored actresses, the girl we had chosen was the best one in the field.

The play opened to lukewarm reviews and ran for only thirty-seven performances. The main reason for its failure, and for the reviews it got, was the performance our leading lady gave. It was sincere, it was the very best of which she was capable, but it was still completely wooden and at times hilariously funny in the wrongest of wrong places. It was much too late to do anything about it, but we suddenly realized that had we braved the bugaboo of casting a white actress in the part, we might in the long run have been much better off. We certainly could not have had a greater failure. In any case here was another lesson for me. In the future I would know better than to invest in Shakespeare, musicals, or plays about colored people. I was beginning to learn about the theater the hard way.

I didn't know it then, but *Black Boy* was to be my last venture as a theatrical angel. The founding of Covici, Friede, the depression that came almost immediately afterward, the attempts to keep my head above water—all these things were to take up entirely too much of my energy and of my money. I still had the Antheil *Ballet Mécanique* ahead of me. But my short and disastrous career as a backer of plays had come to an end.

I did have the feeling, however, that I was somehow associated with the production of *An American Tragedy*, the only play out of which Liveright ever made money. It was more an association by osmosis than in any other way, but I had been connected with the publication of the book, and I was on the scene as our publishing offices turned into theatrical offices in connection with the casting and production of this play. It had a large cast, and for months the reception room was crowded from morning to night with aspiring actors and actresses. Besides, I always remembered that I had had a chance to buy into it, and in time I came to feel that I actually had.

And then there was the incident of the coffee that Dreiser threw at Liveright in the main dining-room at the Ritz. That concerned me very directly, because it came about through a disagreement between Dreiser and Liveright over the sale of the motion-picture rights to *An American Tragedy*, and because I shared in the money Paramount paid for those rights. Fortunately for me I was not present at the luncheon table when Dreiser, infuriated by what he felt was a deliberate attempt on Liveright's part to cheat him, picked up his coffee cup and threw the contents in Liveright's face. If I had been, I would not have had the experience of handling all contacts between Dreiser and the firm of Boni & Liveright for almost a year, for he refused to deal with anyone else for practically that entire time.

And I also would not have had the really unforgettable experience of taking Dreiser to see the play version of his book. He had been in Europe when the play opened, and I had reserved seats for him for the night of his return. I sat next to him, watching his reactions as the story he had created was unfolded on the stage before him. He sat there massively, intensely, as completely absorbed by the play as if all of it were something he was seeing and hearing for the first time. The handkerchief, which it was his invariable habit to fold neatly into an accordion pattern that he would then release only to refold it at once and again and again, was soon a limp and twisted thing. He would not get up in the intermission. He would not talk. He just sat there. And when the curtain went down on the death-cell scene he turned to me, and I could see that there were tears in his eyes. "The poor boy!" he said. "The poor bastard! What a shame!"

FLOP
MÉCANIQUE

$\mathcal{T}$HE Antheil *Ballet Mécanique* was my final venture as a promoter. It was Lewis Galantière who suggested it. There had been a party at my apartment—this was in December of 1926—and sometime during the evening Aaron Copland had played the *Sonata Sauvage* excerpt from the George Antheil supplement to *This Quarter*, the *avant-garde* magazine Ernest Walsh was publishing in Milan. Even on my baby piano—which, because I was then busily collecting modern first editions, had been built into a far wall in an arch of bookcases—it sounded exciting.

"Why don't you bring Antheil over?" Galantiere said. "There must be thousands of people who want to hear his *Ballet Mécanique*. I'll bet you could even fill Carnegie Hall."

"I'd like to hear it myself," I said. "Do you know where we can reach him?"

"He's probably in Paris now," Galantiere said. "And if he isn't, Sylvia Beach will know where to reach him. Why don't you cable him in care of her bookshop? She'll see that he gets it."

It didn't bother either of us that I knew absolutely nothing about putting on a concert, and very little about music. I was a publisher, and as a publisher I had sponsored art exhibits and produced plays. Why not, therefore, a concert? We sat down and drafted a cable to Antheil on the spot. I offered him his expenses for himself and his wife if they would come to America for an all-Antheil concert sometime in April. Any profits were to go to him. I wanted nothing but the fun and the glory.

I got an answer from him three days later. It came from Budapest, where the cable had finally caught up with him. He accepted my proposition and was ready to leave as soon as transportation was forthcoming. And so began the saga of the American première of the *Ballet Mécanique*, which packed Carnegie Hall to overflowing in the spring of 1927. From the very beginning it was fantastic.

The first thing to do was to get the hall. That was a simple matter. Within twenty-four hours I had booked it for Sunday night, April 10th. It had always been a publishing axiom that the best day on which to break a story was on a Monday when the papers were hard put to fill their columns with news. Which is why I picked Sunday night. That was probably the only intelligent move I made.

With Carnegie booked I arranged steamship accommodations for the Antheils for late February. And then I set out to lay my plans for a publicity campaign that would put the concert over.

The fact that I had never had anything to do with any musical event did not bother me for one moment. Publicity was publicity, I told myself, and I knew plenty about that. No firm was as adept in this field as Boni & Liveright, and I meant simply to apply their methods to a different medium. However I did recognize the fact that I needed someone who could act as liaison between myself and the musical critics. For this purpose I engaged Dorle Jarmel, and in the next few months I came to lean on her heavily

45

and was increasingly grateful to have her by my side.

Now I had Carnegie and I had an assistant. The next problem was to plan the program and engage the necessary musicians. William Murray, later the husband of Ilka Chase and a top radio agent, was at that time the New York head of the Baldwin Piano Company. I turned to him for help. And I certainly got it. I knew that the *Ballet Mécanique* was scored for an incredible collection of instruments—how incredible I was to find out later. But the base was a battery of ten regular grand pianos and a mechanical grand. Bill solved that problem immediately. In exchange for the usual "Baldwin Pianos used exclusively" I was promised all I needed whenever I needed them. And, again through Bill Murray, the Welte-Mignon people agreed to supply a player piano incorporating any changes that might have to be made to accommodate the special piano rolls Antheil was mailing me. It turned out that they had to build a practically new mechanism to live up to their promise. But they did not know that then.

With this much taken care of and with the concert still more than three months away, I decided I needed a rest to prepare myself for the hard work to come. I booked passage on the *Reliance* for a two weeks' West Indies cruise. I have often wondered what the radio operator thought of the strange messages which went back and forth during the next fourteen days. They must have confirmed his feeling that all Americans were crazy.

I came back to New York to find that Dorle had things well in hand. We sat down and discussed our plans at length. Since this was to be a benefit concert with all the profits going to Antheil, we decided to sell the lower-tier boxes for a hundred and ten dollars, scaling the house down from there to seventy-five cents for the balcony seats, so that the Greenwich Village *aficionados* would get a chance to hear the concert too. The selling of the boxes was put in the hands of a lady who specialized in such things. Within a week hundreds of beautiful facsimile letters were on their way to the very select sucker list that was her stock in trade. She managed to make it seem a privilege to be permitted to buy one of the boxes. But the letters must have lacked something. Altogether we sold only six boxes at the announced price.

By now I was receiving a constant stream of letters from Antheil, detailed ones suggesting the program he proposed to give, or giving the composition of the musical assistance he would require, copies of the various scores, photographs, publicity matter, all manner of things that would be of assistance to me. His friends were writing me too, voluminous letters filled with their suggestions. I could for instance count on at least one letter from Ezra Pound in each transatlantic mail. They were wonderful too and exciting reading. Unfortunately they were of absolutely no use to us.

It was finally decided that there would be four numbers in the concert: a string quartet, which would be the opening number; a sonata for violin, piano, and drum, with Antheil playing the piano and the drum; and a Jazz Symphony, for which we would require a twenty-three piece orchestra. That would make up the first part of the concert. After the intermission would come the *pièce de résistance*, the *Ballet Mécanique* itself. By now I knew what we would require for this number. In addition to the ten pianos, and ten pianists to play them, and to the mechanical piano, which would be played by Antheil himself, we needed six xylophones, two bass drums, and a variety of mechanical effects. These included a set of electric bells, a wind machine, and for the final climactic moment of the concert, a fire siren.

We could not make out from Antheil's letters just how these mechanical devices were to be constructed, so we decided to wait until he arrived before we did anything about them. But everything else seemed simple enough. We got the Musical Art Quartet, one of the leading groups of the period, without any difficulty. It was agreed that their first violinist, Sascha Jacobsen, would also play the violin in the sonata. We got Eugene Goossens to conduct the *Ballet Mécanique*. We hired six xylophonists and two bass drummers, and we managed to persuade ten very fine pianists, Aaron Copland among them, to help us out by contributing their performances at the ten pianos.

That left the Jazz Symphony. Naturally we tried to get Paul Whiteman, but he was booked solidly, he informed us, and could not possibly co-operate. So we were faced with the really difficult problem of assembling a large orchestra under a suitable conductor for this very difficult piece. It was written in one movement, lasting about fifteen minutes, and it was scored for three saxophones, one oboe, three trumpets, three trombones, one tuba, two banjos, three pianos, four violins, two violas, one 'cello, and one contrabass. I cannot remember who first suggested getting W. C. Handy to conduct, but it struck us as an excellent idea. Surely the man who wrote the *St. Louis Blues* would be a welcome addition to our already exciting group of performers.

Handy was engaged at once and commissioned to form an orchestra. He got together a truly wonderful collection of colored players, men who knew and loved jazz, even though they seemed slightly bewildered by the score they would be required to play. Handy was the least disturbed of any of them. We were to find out the reason for his calmness later.

While all this was going on we were busy planting publicity stories and pictures. Ford Madox Ford wrote an article for *Vanity Fair*, and Lewis Galantière wrote one for the Sunday edition of the *New York World*. Man Ray and

Bernice Abbott photographs of Antheil were made available to any papers or magazines that would use them, and Miguel Covarrubias and William Cotton were standing by to draw caricatures as soon as Antheil landed in America. It was for a while very difficult to pick up a magazine or a feature section of a newspaper without seeing something about our concert.

And then I had another brainstorm. I decided that the classic and ultraconservative background against which Carnegie Hall concerts were played was completely wrong for our purposes. I commissioned Joseph Mullen, the set designer, to execute two backdrops for me, one for the Jazz Symphony and one for the *Ballet Mécanique*. The first two numbers were to be played in front of the house curtain. He produced two sketches that I accepted enthusiastically. For the Jazz Symphony he had conceived a backdrop of a gigantic Negro couple dancing the Charleston, the girl holding an American flag in her left hand, while the man clasped her ecstatically around the buttocks. This backdrop covered the whole rear of the stage from beam to floor. For the *Ballet Mécanique* he had an even more eye-filling idea. It was to be practically a cyclorama with a futuristic city of skyscrapers as a background; and in the foreground a series of enormous noise-making machines: whistles, riveting machines, airplane propellers, spark plugs, excavating machines; and in the left-hand corner a more-than-life-size figure of a man jumping off a diving board that seemed to be attached to a curved pipe of the sort generally used in connection with a toilet. I spent hours during the next month at the theatrical studios where these backdrops were executed.

Antheil arrived in New York early in March. He came on the *Ascania*, a small White Star liner that usually would have been completely passed up by the ships' news reporters. And yet when I went down the bay to meet him,

I found that eight of the top men in the field were on the tug with me. There was no doubt about it: the preliminary publicity had been well done. Antheil and I had never met, and when I saw him on deck and recognized his youthful face from his pictures, I had a difficult time making him believe that I was really the man who was putting on his concert. He had, I gathered, expected me to be an old man with a long white beard instead of someone actually a year younger than his twenty-six. The reporters insisted on his playing some of his music for them, and we went down to the salon where he did the best he could with a typical ship's piano. I could see from the newspapermen's faces that it was not an auspicious introduction.

There were stories in all the papers and on all the news wires the next day. I was not particularly worried about the fact that they were not very flattering. I subscribed completely to the current theory that any publicity was good publicity if they spelled your name right. But there was one editorial, in the *World*, which did disturb me. It condemned Antheil and his music on the basis that there was no melody in modern music, and took the attitude that he deserved no consideration at all since he dealt only in cacophony. I managed to find out that this editorial had been written by James M. Cain, and I called Cain up and invited him to my apartment, where Antheil and his wife were staying, to hear Antheil play. I promised him enough melody to make him change his mind. To my surprise he came. He listened to Antheil's playing for almost an hour, went back to the *World*, and wrote another editorial, taking back everything he had said the previous day. As far as I know, this is unique as a newspaper reversal.

With Antheil on hand things started to move rapidly. We called the first rehearsal of the *Ballet Mécanique* for that afternoon, and we asked the xylophonists and drummers to bring their instruments to Liveright's apartment

for a preliminary run-through of the music. The first rehearsal for the pianists was set for the following morning,
at the Welte-Mignon studios at Fifty-second Street and
Twelfth Avenue. I got to the apartment a little late and
found a very bewildered Antheil trying to persuade eight
hard-boiled union musicians that the music they had before them could actually be played. They were reading it
gleefully to each other, exploding with laughter at anybody's temerity in thinking it made any musical sense at
all. They were completely unaware of the fact that the
very embarrassed and shy young man at the piano was the
composer. I explained this to them as tactfully as I could,
and we managed to get the rehearsal started.

A lot of people had been invited to stop by and meet
Antheil, and they kept coming in during the next hour.
Meanwhile the musicians were manfully trying to go
through the score, minus the ten pianos that were such an
important part of the piece, and with Antheil doing his
best to play the mechanical-piano part for them and to
hum the sections of the score for which the instruments
were lacking. It was not altogether successful as a rehearsal. It was even less of a success as part of a cocktail
party. The noise in the average-size living-room was deafening, and we were finally requested by the management
to stop it at once. Everybody in the house, it seemed, was
complaining. There were only a few pages of the score left
to play when the call came from downstairs, and Liveright
told us to ignore it and to finish the rehearsal. It must be
remembered that in those days you still had your choice of
apartments, and landlords had not yet become idols to be
placated with burnt offerings. So we ignored the request to
stop, and the rehearsal went on to its bitter end. And bitter
indeed it was. All through the previous hour there had
been a constant tinkling sound coming, we soon discovered,
from a pane of glass in one of the windows that vibrated in

unison with one of the bass drums. Now as we came to the crashing finale of the *Ballet*, which was to include every instrument in the orchestra as well as all of the mechanical effects, the constant vibration proved too much for the windowpane. With the final notes from the six xylophones, the two bass drums, and the piano, it crashed into a thousand pieces, and we could hear it tinkling on the ground in the courtyard as it fell. That ended our rehearsals in apartments.

The first rehearsal of the pianists the next morning went much better. The eleven grand pianos made a magnificent picture in the huge Welte-Mignon studios, and Goossen's practiced hand quickly made order out of chaos. The xylophonists and drummers recognized his authority at once, and it was soon obvious to all of us that we would have no trouble at all with this number. Even the mechanical problems proved to be not too difficult. We found an electrician who undertook to make the battery of electric bells that we needed. We commissioned a wind machine with a regulation airplane propeller. And we started our search for a real fire siren. We all breathed a sigh of relief after the rehearsal. It wasn't going to be so very difficult after all, we told ourselves.

We were even more cocky after the rehersal with the string quartet, and later with Jacobsen and Antheil playing the sonata. Here were accomplished musicians functioning together as accomplished musicians miraculously do, and we knew that we need have no worries in connection with these two numbers either.

But the Jazz Symphony was a different matter. We moved the mechanical piano and seven of the other pianos to the far end of the Welte-Mignon studios, and we set up the three pianos and the stands for the twenty other players. Handy had assembled a really fine orchestra, and we looked forward to an exciting performance of an exciting number. We handed the score to Handy and distributed the parts to the other men. And then we sat back to listen.

Three rehearsals later we were still listening, but as yet we had heard nothing that even vaguely resembled the symphony that Antheil had written. We were completely puzzled. Here was a fine group of musicians, led by a man whose name was a musical byword. And yet he did not seem able to do anything about pulling them together and making them play the music that stood before them on the stands. It took us two more rehearsals, at union-scale wages of course, to figure out this deepening mystery.

The answer, when we finally got it, was ridiculously simple. Handy, for all his great musical ability, could not cope with the fantastic intricacies of Antheil's score. It is quite probable that if he had ever heard the Jazz Symphony played he could have done an excellent job of conducting it, and even of teaching it to his orchestra. But it was a new composition, radical in form and content to boot. And it was simply beyond him.

He made no objection when we told him we would have to get another conductor. He understood our problem perfectly. He promised to do all he could to help us. But we still were faced with the problem of finding his substitute.

We were fortunate in getting a very good man almost at once. And again the rehearsals started. But we were suddenly faced with a new problem: we could not continue to clutter up the Welte-Mignon studios with eleven grand pianos. Again Bill Murray was most co-operative. The Baldwin people would be only too happy to put a truck and a crew of men at our disposal. All we had to do was to let him know in the morning where we wanted the pianos set up, and they would be there waiting for us when we wanted them. I have always been fascinated since then by the thought that there was once a time in my life when I had only to lift a phone and eleven grand pianos would start moving toward any place I wanted them to go.

It was soon obvious that the Jazz Symphony would need a great many rehearsals, many, many more than we had counted on. Actually there were finally twenty-five. Most of the later ones took place in Harlem in the hospitable home of Alelia Walker, the daughter and heir of the woman who had invented the most effective method of hair-straightening that had yet been thought of. She was delighted to have us meet in the ballroom of her house day after day, complete with our grand pianos and our twenty other instruments. And gradually the symphony took form. Finally we knew definitely that we need not worry about that number either.

There was another thing we had no worries about. Carnegie Hall, excepting for the lower-tier boxes, was sold out within twenty-four hours of the time the tickets were placed on sale. And I had the bright idea of using the unsold boxes for the complimentary tickets I had to dispense so lavishly. After all, I had to give tickets to everybody at Boni & Liveright and to all our authors and to all the literary critics, not to mention the musical critics. As a matter of fact I found the night of the concert that I had been too lavish. There were not enough seats in all the boxes to take care of the people who had been invited. However, the solution was very simple. I had extra seats put in. But I forgot to tell the ushers to be sure not to place any in the six boxes that had actually been sold. These boxholders were none too happy to suddenly find the best seats pre-empted by people they were certain they had never before met socially. It took quite a bit of work on my part to make them feel better.

But that was still in the future. In the last few crowded weeks before the concert the publicity build-up was coming to a climax. It was a hectic period, made doubly so by the constant round of parties. Everybody wanted to meet Antheil, and I doubt if there were five nights during his entire stay here when we did not end up in some large gathering. Two of these parties were really memorable.

There was the night we all went up to Theodore Dreiser's enormous studio on Fifty-seventh Street. As usual the huge living-room was crowded with the excitingly heterogeneous group who came to these weekly gatherings, a form of open house presided over by the massive gray-haired Dreiser sitting in a thronelike chair that towered above his head, eternally folding and unfolding the handkerchief he held in his left hand. He refused to take the boyish looking Antheil seriously. Nobody this young, he said, could possibly be entitled to all the fantastic things that had been said about him. But he was willing to be convinced. He called for silence, and when he got it he turned to Antheil. "Go on," he said, "play. Let's see what this is all about." And Antheil played—for almost an hour as I remember it. When he had finished, Dreiser looked at him and smiled. "I take it all back," he said. "Sit down here and talk to me." And in the deeply probing way that was almost uniquely his, Dreiser talked to him until the last guest had gone, asking endless questions as if to assimilate all the knowledge and all the ideas Antheil had managed to acquire.

The other party took place at my apartment. I had been approached the previous week by one of the saxophonists in the orchestra that Handy had assembled for us. "I understand," he said, "that you're giving a lot of parties for Mr. Antheil." That was true, I said. "And," he continued, "there are lots of important musical people at these parties." Yes, I said, there were. "Well, would you mind," he asked, "if I brought my choir to sing for you at your next party? I have a chorus of thirty-five voices, and we do a lot of singing in Harlem. It would be a great thing for us if we could sing for some of the critics." I would be delighted, I assured him. We set the date for the following week.

I had twenty-five guests that night, chosen for their interest in things musical. The choir brought the number of people in my not over-large living-room to almost seventy. We sat at one end of the room, and the singers ranged themselves against the far wall. And then they started to sing. The windows shook, the pictures on the walls trembled, and I wondered fleetingly if the experience in Liveright's apartment was to be duplicated. I say fleetingly, for after a very few minutes I didn't care. I had never heard spirituals sung so beautifully, and my guests seemed to agree. They would not let the choir stop. They sang until they were exhausted. And so were we, from the beauty and power the saxophonist—his name, by the way, was Hall Johnson—had managed to instill into his group.

And all through these mad days of rehearsals and interviews and parties Antheil drifted in a daze, unable fully to absorb everything that was going on around him. He was completely amenable to anything I suggested, overcome, as I later found out, by my sheer exuberance and cocksureness. He didn't even complain very much when he found that my piano had been carefully tuned one half tone off key by the piano tuner who came up the day before he arrived from Europe. He was much too mild and inexperienced to argue. And I did give the impression of knowing exactly what I was doing. The trouble was that I was doing for a musical event what I would normally do for a book. And I did not realize that one by one I was alienating all the critics, all the people who were really important to him, all the people who had contributed toward making it possible for him to write his music without any financial worries, by turning a serious performance into a circus.

To top it all it became increasingly obvious that there

would not be any profits. The twenty-five rehearsals of the Jazz Symphony would have been enough to make that point certain. And the backdrops took their disproportionate share of the receipts. Even with a sold-out house, excepting, of course, for the lower-tier boxes, there would be a big loss. This meant that Antheil would have made the trip and given the concert for his expenses only. I tried not to think to what besides experience I could charge the losses I would have to bear.

But finally the day of the concert came around. We had scheduled a final dress rehearsal in Carnegie Hall for ten in the morning. We had to be finished by two so that the stage could be reset for the afternoon Philharmonic concert. We hung the backdrops, set up the wind machine, rehearsed the stage crew and the piano movers—old friends of ours now after weeks of shifting pianos hundreds of blocks each day—and ran through the whole concert. Everything went beautifully. We could not imagine how there could be any hitches. We went home to rest until evening.

There was one thing, however, that still bothered us a little. We had as yet not been able to secure a fire siren. Every time we had reached the climactic point in the *Ballet Mécanique* when it was supposed to come in, the very capable man who operated our mechanical devices would go through the motions of cranking an imaginary fire siren. This had not been particularly satisfactory, but it was the best we could do. In any case we were sure we had nothing to worry about. One of the xylophonists had a brother who was connected with the fire department in a small New Jersey town right across the river. In exchange for two tickets—lower-tier box seats of course—he solemnly swore that he would bring a genuine fire siren to us that night in plenty of time for it to be set up on its appointed stand.

When we got back to Carnegie Hall after the Philharmonic concert was over, we found that he had kept his word. There was the siren, shiny and red, and we mounted it on its stand at once. And we struck the backdrop that had been used for the afternoon's concert, rehung our cyclorama and our backdrop, set up our wind machine, and grouped the seven pianos and the mechanical piano, which would not be used until the second half of the concert, back of the backdrop for the Jazz Symphony, where they would not be in the way. We set up the instruments and the stands for the Jazz Symphony safely back of the house curtain, and then we lowered the curtain and set up the chairs and the stands for the string quartet in front of the curtain. It was probably the most elaborate setup for a concert that had ever been devised.

By the time we were through, the audience was beginning to come into the theater. I went out into the lobby, and was astonished to find it jammed with hundreds of people who were desperately trying to buy tickets. All the standing-room tickets had long ago been sold out, and the holders of these formed a solid mass at the rear of the orchestra and flowed down into the aisles, far deeper than I had ever seen them at any other concert. I found out later that the printers had made a mistake and had printed three times as many standing-room tickets as had been ordered. A number of orchestra seats had fallen into the hands of speculators, and they were having no difficulty at all in disposing of them. One thing I could be sure of: for whatever it was worth I had certainly managed to fill "even Carnegie Hall" to suffocation.

The concert itself was a complete anticlimax. The minute the string quaret started to play I realized that we had made a hideously bad choice of an opening number. Played against the deadening house curtain, it was completely lost in the vast reaches of the hall. The same was true of the sonata that followed, except that Antheil's practically simultaneous playing of the piano and the drum brought on a wave of amusement that threatened for a while to drown out what little of the music could be heard. And when the curtain went up on the orchestra in front of the billowing, buttocksy backdrop of the colossal Charleston, the audience roared with laughter. I had not realized how utterly incongruous it would seem to use such a backdrop in hallowed Carnegie Hall. I sat miserably in my box. I thought of all that I should have done, and wondered why I had ever let myself in for this agony.

I felt better a few minutes later. The audience liked the Jazz Symphony and greeted its conclusion with the first real applause of the evening. I hurried backstage (where I should have been all along) to suggest to the orchestra that they repeat the number. But I was too late. The curtain had been rung down, and the stage hands were getting to work setting up the pianos for the *Ballet Mécanique*. The backdrop for the previous number was raised and the cyclorama adjusted. And then we discovered that we had miscalculated the space that would be available to us, and so instead of being able to set the stage discreetly back of the lowered curtain, we had to raise the curtain and work in full view of the highly amused audience. It spoiled the dramatic impact we had counted on: the raising of the curtain on the full depth of the Carnegie Hall stage, with the eleven pianos and all the other instruments grouped in front of the really effective cyclorama that seemed to give it added depth. Instead, word got around in the lobby that there were strange doings to be seen inside, and for the next ten minutes the entire audience sat in its seats, watching heaving piano movers jockeying grand pianos into a huge semicircle, while electricians hooked up a full size airplane propeller on a high stand at the left of the conductor's podium, and other electricians set up rows of electric bells and a bright-red fire siren on a wooden pedestal.

It was a bad introduction to the number, but worse was to follow. The first few minutes of the *Ballet* went off smoothly, and the audience listened to it carefully. And then came the moment for the wind machine to be turned on—and all hell, in a minor way, broke loose. Someone had made a mistake, and instead of having the propeller point into the air, where the breeze it would generate would be dissipated before it reached the back of the house, it now was aimed at a point in the eleventh row of the orchestra. While it gathered speed nothing happened, but when it reached its full power it was disastrous. People clutched their programs, and women held onto their hats with both hands. Someone in the direct line of the wind tied a handkerchief to his cane and waved it wildly in the air in a sign of surrender. It was impossible to readjust the wind machine while the music continued, and impossible to stop the music to readjust the wind machine. The man in charge of the mechanical effects did the only thing that could be done. He turned the machine down to a point where it would not blow the poor people in the eleventh row out of their seats, and hoped for the best.

But the damage had been done. Laughter is contagious, and besides we had spent weeks building up the fact that there had been riots in Paris at the first performance of this number. Now everybody—to quote the great Durante —wanted to get into the act. The riot they put on, however, was completely synthetic. Goossens turned to glare at the noisemakers, and they shut up at once. But then the more conservative members of the audience decided that they had had enough. They started to leave in droves. It was an agonizing experience for Antheil, and I, back in my box once more, could not help but feel for him. I knew he wished, as I did most fervently, that we had never heard of each other.

The *Ballet* finally drew to a close. At this point every instrument on the stage was playing, and the noise was terrific. And now came the moment for the fire siren to sound. Goossens gave the cue, and the mechanical-effects man turned the crank wildly, while the audience, unable to contain itself any longer, burst once more into uncontrolled laughter. But there was no sound from the siren. He turned the crank more and more wildly, and still there was no sound. The moment for the siren was by now long past, and Goossens was turning to the last page of the score. Disgustedly the effects man stopped turning the crank, as the last bars of the *Ballet* crashed out. And then in the silence that followed there came the unmistakable sounds of a fire siren gathering speed. Louder and louder it came as the last notes of the *Ballet* died away, and as Goossens turned to bow to the audience and Antheil rose from the piano, it reached its full force. We had all of us completely forgotten the simple fact that a fire siren does not start making any sound until it has been energetically cranked for almost a full minute. And also we had forgotten that it does not stop shrieking simply because you stop cranking. We remembered both of these things now as the wail from the infernal red thing on the stage kept dinning in our ears, drowning out the applause of the audience, covering the sound of the people picking up their coats and hats and leaving the auditorium.

I got up to go backstage again. As I came out of my box I ran into a friend of mine, a wit in high standing at the Round Table in the Algonquin. "Too bad, Donald," he said. "You tried to make a mountain out of an Antheil." I managed a mechanical smile.

THE
FLYING
FOOL

I SAILED for Europe a few days after the concert, taking the Antheils with me. If it had not been for the fact that I had booked passage long before that fateful evening, I might have been accused of running away. Certainly I wanted to forget everything about it, and I'm sure Antheil did too.

It was he who suggested that I stay at Foyot's, that fabulous hotel around the corner from the Senate, whose memory still brings tears to the eyes of the true gourmet. The restaurant was unquestionably the finest of which Paris ever boasted, and I have always suspected Antheil of getting me to stay there because he knew that in that way we would be likely to dine there more often than if I lived elsewhere. Actually the restaurant itself was the main reason for Foyot's. The hotel proper consisted of a lobby and twelve rooms. There were also two suites, and I was to stay in them both often in the next few years. My favorite was the one that reminded me of nothing so much as a New York railroad flat. It consisted of a long private hall with four rooms, a living-room, two bedrooms, and a bath-

room, all opening off it. It was dark, it was not particularly
well furnished, but it had one advantage that made it seem
perfection itself in my eyes: I had only to pick up the
phone and a breakfast, lunch, or dinner would appear from
the restaurant downstairs, finer than anything I had ever
dreamed of, perfectly served and miraculously hot. I never
stayed anywhere else in Paris until Foyot's closed its doors
for good late in the depression.

But in 1927 there was no thought of depression in Paris
or anywhere else. The Parisians were getting ready for
the summer rush of tourists, and it was predicted that it
would be the biggest invasion of all time. And the expatriate colony was increasing daily. It had almost reached
its peak then, and the Dôme, the Coupole, and the Rotonde
were packed solidly day and night with Americans whose
only idea of a fate worse than death was to have to return
to America. And the franc, to their great satisfaction, continued to drop. They were all, no matter how small their
incomes, exchange-rich.

It was early in May when I got there, and the papers
were full of news of the proposed flights for the Orteig
twenty-five-thousand-dollar prize. The very shrewd owner
of the Brevoort and Lafayette hotels in New York had
posted this amount some years before as a reward for the
first flyer to make a nonstop trip between New York and
Paris. The interest he had collected on this money in the
intervening years had undoubtedly cut his investment considerably. And besides he had had many times twenty-five
thousand dollars' worth of publicity. Now it finally began
to look as if he might be called on to turn over the money
to someone for having succeeded in living up to the terms
he had set.

There had already been one crash of an entrant's plane
this year. The *American Legion*, backed by Richard Hoyt
the Wall Street specialist in aviation stocks, had come

down in flames on its first test flight, killing both of the men who had planned to fly it across the Atlantic. Now there was to be another tragedy, and for a while it seemed this one might have serious repercussions.

By the terms of the Orteig prize the flight could be made either from east to west or from west to east. Mostly the entrants were Americans, planning to fly from New York. But there was one pair of French flyers, Nungesser and Coli, who were going to make the attempt in the other direction. They took off from Paris on May 8th and were never heard from again, although it was reported, and with some degree of credibility, that their plane had been sighted over Newfoundland the following day.

When they did take off, and while it was still possible that they might actually complete the flight successfully, Paris went wild. Here, Frenchmen said to themselves, was a chance for one of them to show these cocky Americans a thing or two. Had not another Frenchman only the previous fall won the United States Tennis Championship from the supposedly invincible Americans? True the Davis Cup was still in America, but things would be different this year. And on a different level too it was hoped by many that the prize would be won by a Frenchman: the Supreme Court of the state of Massachusetts had just ruled that Sacco and Vanzetti must die, and American popularity in France had hit an all-time low.

Besides all this, Nungesser was a wartime ace of aces and personally one of the most popular men in France. When it finally became obvious to even the most optimistic of optimists that he and Coli were lost, and probably for good, there was a sudden and noticeable change in temper. This, the feeling seemed to be, was the last straw. The fact that the prize had been offered by a Frenchman was completely overlooked. All that stood out clearly was that a great French flyer had been sacrificed, and that nothing now seemed to stand in the way of an American's winning the prize. And the almost unanimous choice for this honor was Commander Richard Evelyn Byrd, who, it was felt, would probably have already completed the flight if it had not been for an accident to his plane on one of its final test flights. He had, however, announced that he expected to be ready to start very soon.

It was at this precise moment that the name of Lindbergh first started to appear in the Paris papers. I had read of him a month or so earlier in the *New York Times*— they had spelled his name Linberg—when it was announced that he was about to begin test flights of a Ryan plane that had been built for him in San Diego. All that the *Times* knew about him was that he was an ex-mail flyer, and it hinted strongly at the fact that what he was after was publicity. Now it was announced that he had completed his tests and had then flown across the country to Mineola to join the other planes that were warming up for the flight to Paris.

There was something about the idea of anyone, even an American, attempting a solo flight across the Atlantic that caught the fancy of the French. Or maybe it was that they wondered, with true Gallic directness, how he would be able to do certain things that, even if performed in public lavatories, still required more concentration than could be given them by someone who was completely occupied in keeping an airplane in the air. In any case, in the eight days that elapsed between the time Lindbergh landed at Mineola and the time he took off for Paris, there was another reversal of opinion. True, Nungesser and Coli had been given up for lost. It was indeed a shame that those two brave men had perished. But what would you? Those were the fortunes of war. This Lindbergh though! That was really something. It was to be hoped that he would make it safely.

When he finally took off on May 20th all of Paris was pulling for him. Everybody wanted to bet, and it was a strange fact that all of France seemed to want to bet that he would complete the flight successfully. It was the Americans who were doubtful. They apparently refused to believe that one man alone in a plane with only one engine could do what all the others were planning to do in groups and in multimotored planes. It was a complete refutation of the American genius for building complicated machines. I could have made a lot of money taking my compatriots' bets. The trouble was that I was very doubtful about it myself.

But I was no longer doubtful the following evening. We had been eagerly grabbing every extra that came out—and they came out almost every hour—and as yet there had not been one single confirmed report that Lindbergh's plane had actually been sighted anywhere along the line. Yet there was a growing feeling that he would land that night at Le Bourget, and I shared it fully. We had dinner with the Antheils that night, at Foyot's naturally, and he and I tried to persuade our wives to come out to the airport with us. They only scoffed at us. It was ridiculous, they said. He would never arrive. If he wasn't already in the middle of the ocean, surely someone would have seen him. No, we could go if we wanted to. They would meet us at Ciro's later.

The roads to Le Bourget, we found when we started out for it in a taxi, were black with traffic. Seemingly thousands of other people had the same confidence in Lindbergh that we had. We crawled along for three times the time it should have taken us to get there. Finally we got out of our cab almost a full mile from the entrance to the field and walked the rest of the way. It was good that we did. The blockade that had immobilized us in one spot for almost an hour was caused, we found, by the fact that the thrifty French taxi drivers had figured out that everybody who was going to Le Bourget would want to get back too, and only after Lindbergh had landed or had been given up for lost. So they had locked their cabs by the thousands and gone off to join the crowds back of the fences around the field.

Fortunately Antheil had a police card, and this made it possible for us to go to the roof of the Administration Building, where there were only a few hundred people, instead of having to stand in the suffocating crowd on the ground. It was the biggest crowd I have ever seen in my life, and the most completely intent. We all faced to the north and stared at the sky, hoping to be the first to see the flash of a plane's wings in the beam of the pointing search-lights.

It was about an hour after we got there that Lindbergh landed. There had been two or three false alarms, and we were temporarily off guard, when there was a sudden surging forward in the crowd below us, and the sound of a hundred thousand voices coming abruptly out of the stillness. And as we watched the plane glide gently onto the field, we saw the mob begin to rush madly onto the field and toward it. We could hear fences giving way and the shrieks of men and women as the crowds back of them pushed them forward into the unyielding mass ahead of them. Suddenly the field was full of people running, and almost before the plane had come to a stop they were around it, tearing at it, ripping at the wings, trying to reach inside and get at Lindbergh. It was some time before the police could form a ring around the plane and get him out.

In the meantime the crowd on the roof had gone wild too. We were pounding each other on the back, trying to make ourselves heard above the din. One Frenchman made a point of coming up to us and shaking us solemnly by the hand. "You should be proud," he said, "to be Americans." We assured him we were. We shook his hand just as solemnly and all had a drink from the flask of brandy we had brought with us.

We never did get to see Lindbergh. Or at least I do not think we did. From the top of the stairs we saw a very disheveled young man being helped through a crowd that seemed intent on tearing him to pieces. We were certain that was he but were told later that it was just an accommodating young man who had agreed to impersonate Lindbergh and thus help draw the crowd away from its prey. Still later we heard that it had actually been Lindbergh himself. I never managed to find out which story was true.

It took us even longer to get back to Paris than it had taken us to get to the field. But we didn't care. We were exhausted by the excitement. When we joined our wives at Ciro's they glared at us reproachfully, as if it had been our fault that they had not been at Le Bourget with us. We had to be very tactful with them.

I was at the Guaranty Trust the following day seeing one of the vice-presidents of the bank, and naturally we talked about the flight. He had been at the field too, and was in the process of arranging a welcoming luncheon for Lindbergh at the American Club, of which he was an official. "Want to meet him?" he asked. "I can get you to him easily. And you're the only publisher in Paris right now. Maybe you'd like to talk about a book."

I laughed. "A book by Lindbergh?" I said. "No thanks. He'll be forgotten in six months."

In the next few years, as I watched *We* go right to the top of the best-seller list and stay there, I was to remember that remark with increasing bitterness. As a matter of fact, when I came back to New York on the day of the official reception for Lindbergh, and saw the bay full of ships out to greet him, and planes flying overhead, and crowds lining Broadway hours before the parade was to start, I could have kicked myself for having made such a fantastic mistake. In spite of the almost hysterical excitement all about me, I refused to leave the house all day. I was mad clear through.

THE
BOY
GROWS
OLDER

I THINK I can safely say that no book that I ever turned down achieved the sale of *We*. One of the reasons is, of course, that very few books have ever sold as many copies as this phenomenal best seller finally did. But Paris was to be the scene of another debacle for me, and less than eight months after my cavalier dismissal of Charles A. Lindbergh. It all came about when I decided to go there to have lunch with James Joyce.

The purpose of my trip was to secure the publishing rights to Joyce's new and not yet completed book. I was also going to attempt to sell him on the idea of letting us fight the case for *Ulysses* in the courts. It was my feeling that we could win the case and thus be able to publish *Ulysses* openly in America. I booked a round-trip passage on the S. S. *Paris* and set out on my journey.

I was, I thought, well fortified. *Work in Progress*, as it was then known, was being pirated in at least one magazine, each section appearing as soon as practicable after its appearance in Paris in *transition*. Elliot Paul and Eugene

Jolas had enlisted my aid on Joyce's behalf, and I had set up the first quarter of the book at my own expense, printing fifteen copies only for the sole purpose of securing the American copyright for Joyce. I had a copy of the book with me, and a signed contract for Joyce, and the promise of a substantial monthly payment to make to him. It would have meant security for life for him, and when I got off the *Paris* at Le Havre, leaving my laundry to be done while the ship was in harbor, to be picked up by me when I boarded the ship again for the return trip to New York three days later, I was full of high hopes.

I was a very much disillusioned man a few days later as I watched the shores of France recede. For the first and only time in my life I had been the victim of an organized conspiracy. I had ended by losing my shirt on the *Ballet Mécanique*, and Antheil got nothing for his time and trouble, except his expenses and occasional advances for pocket money. And he took a terrible critical lambasting as well. It took time for Antheil to realize how seriously the Carnegie Hall fiasco had affected his entire musical career— among other things, Mrs. Bok, outraged by the circus treatment I had given the whole affair, had withdrawn the subsidy on which he had been living—but when he did he naturally, and I must say justifiably, came to hate me for what I had caused to happen to him. He hated me so very much that a few years later, under a nom de plume, he wrote a detective story about me, in the opening pages of which he had the reader discover me dead in bed, a knife stuck in my back. In the balance of the book he managed to kill off my mother, my wife, and my brother, as well as a psychiatrist whom he had met through me. It was a very thorough job and had excellent cathartic results, as our present friendship proves.

But when I arrived in Paris to see Joyce, Antheil had not yet written the book, and his hatred of me was in full flower. He was very close to all the people around Joyce and to Joyce himself. And he had managed to convey the impression that I was an unmitigated rascal who was under no circumstances to be trusted. So well had he done his job, as a matter of fact, that I found it impossible at first to even get to see Joyce, and I faced the ridiculous chance that I might have made a six-thousand-mile trip in vain. Finally I got Elliot Paul, the editor of *transition*, to intercede for me, and it was he who went to Joyce to ask him to see me. He took along, as an earnest of my good faith, the bound copy of the book I had brought over for Joyce.

Through Paul an appointment with Joyce was finally arranged. That, I was certain, was all that was needed. The contract I had brought with me, the money I was prepared to offer him, the substantial proof of my activities on his behalf, which must be concretely evident to him on the basis of the volume Paul had given him the day before—all these things, I thought, would be quite sufficient to make Joyce realize I had been maligned and slandered. I was all smiles when I was shown into Joyce's study by Mrs. Joyce, and shook hands with the cadaverous man with the inch-thick spectacles.

Fifteen minutes later I shook hands with him again and was politely ushered out of the room by Mrs. Joyce. I had been given no opportunity to present the contract I had with me, no chance to tell Joyce that if he accepted our offer he need never worry about money again. Instead Joyce had turned to the copyright page of the volume I had brought over from New York, and had icily pointed out that the copyright seemed to have been taken out in my name. On whose authority, he wanted to know, had this been done? It was a mere formality, I assured him, a method of protecting his rights until I was officially empowered to act for him. The copyright could be transferred to him at any time. Could I do it now? he asked. Unfortunately, I replied, it could not be done until I got back to America. I had not brought copies of the necessary form with me. They would be executed as soon as I got back to New York, and would then be mailed to him at once. In that case, he said, would I mind making the subject of the conversation I had planned to have with him an accompanying letter to this transfer of copyright? He would be glad to read it carefully then, and he would write me his decision. In the meantime he would have to ask to be excused. He was a very busy man. He stood up and put out his hand.

I came back to New York completely deflated. It was probably the most resounding defeat of my whole life. I executed the transfer of copyright and mailed Joyce his copy of the document. In my covering letter I said only that I enclosed the transfer he had asked for. I did not bother to mention the contract we had wanted to offer him or the advance we had been prepared to pay.

But my hurt feelings were soon forgotten in the rush of things that happened right after my return. Less than a week after I got back, I handed Liveright my resignation from Boni & Liveright and sold him back all my stock holdings in the company. There had been increasing friction between us, and I felt that the time had come for me to go out on my own. I would start my own publishing house.

And the spring of 1928 was a perfect time for dreams of plenty and of glory unlimited. The final fantastic spiraling of the stock market still had a year and a half to go— U. S. Steel was a full hundred points short of the record high of 261¾ it was to reach—Lindbergh had just received the Congressional Medal of Honor and had then flown down to Mexico City, where one of his first passengers was Dwight W. Morrow—the tabloids had just printed the picture of Ruth Snyder in the electric chair—Trotsky, Kamenev, Zinoviev, and Radek were banished by the Soviet government, and the papers were full of stories prophesying the imminent end of Communism in Russia—C. C. Pyle's "Bunion Derby" was making its painful way across the nation—the manuscript of *Alice in Wonderland* was bought by Dr. Rosenbach for $77,260—Sir Joseph Duveen bought a Gainsborough for $360,000—a bust by Houdon brought $245,000 at auction—Gene Tunney lectured on Shakespeare before William Lyon Phelps's class at Yale—Walter May and his wife took sixty-four friends from Pittsburgh to Paris for their silver wedding anniversary dinner—Carol of Roumania arrived in England with Mme. Lupescu and was deported six days later—Raphael's *Madonna and Child* brought $875,000 in London—twenty-four New York theater-ticket speculators were fined $5,000 each—260 plays opened on Broadway during the year—and I sold part of my collection of modern first editions for $14,000.

It was, in short, a period of unlimited optimism, the apex of the "Era of Wonderful Nonsense." Calvin Coolidge, in an Indian headdress or posing as a fisherman in a conservative business suit, was about to be succeeded by Herbert Hoover and his impeccably tailored platitudes. War had been outlawed for good and all, television was just around the corner, and the air age was about to flower fully. Prohibition was a joke, and a phone call to your favorite bootlegger, at any time of the day or night, would bring you anything you wanted to drink at prices that were not too exorbitant. Not that it would have mattered too much if they had been: money was the cheapest of all commodities, and the American tourists pouring into France pointed up this by lighting their cigars with hundred-franc notes, thereby endearing themselves to the natives.

The book market too reflected the temper of the times. There were simply not enough books being printed to supply the demand. So many orders were received by Harper's for copies of the limited edition of a new book by Edna Millay that all the orders were dumped into a hat and a well-publicized drawing was held to determine the lucky dealers who would be allotted one copy out of the five or ten or more they had ordered. And when I made my trips on the road as a salesman for Boni & Liveright, the orders I took for black-list books sometimes exceeded my orders for new books. Everybody may not have been reading them, but certainly everybody was buying.

I had always admired the brilliant publishing acumen of Jonathan Cape the London publisher, and I now got in touch with him. I wanted to start an American branch of his house, and I outlined my ideas to him. I felt that the prestige of his name and the ready-made list that would be ours would simplify the basic problem facing all potential publishers, namely where to get their first list. I still remembered the story about Dick Simon and Max Schuster who had gone out to lunch after watching the sign painter put the finishing touches to the sign on the front door of their new offices, a sign that read very simply and starkly: "Simon & Schuster, Publishers," and had come back to find another equally simple sign tacked on the door under the not yet dry gilt of their lettering. "Of What?" asked this sign, and it was a fair question at the time, with their only book a crossword puzzle book with a pencil included at no extra cost.

But Cape was none too enthusiastic. I would have to learn his methods, he wrote. I would have to live in London for a year, working in the office with him, and we would have to see how we got along before we could make any definite plans. The idea of living in London was a most appealing one, but Cape's suggestion that I pay all my

75

expenses and draw no salary during this period was not. The Antheil concert, my disastrous ventures as a theatrical angel, the fact that my deal with Liveright called for the repurchase by him of my stock interest in Boni & Liveright in monthly payments spread out over a number of years—these things had reduced the actual capital at my disposal to a point where I could not possibly consider such a proposition. Besides which I had pretty high ideas about myself and my worth. I turned down his suggestion as, I realized later, he had hoped I would. In view of the fact that he started his American branch house the following year, in partnership with Harrison Smith, it is quite likely that he had his plans well laid even before I first discussed my plan with him.

American publishers were not so coy. I was wooed diligently and ardently by quite a few of them. I had no illusions about what they were after. I was well aware of the fact that they were much more interested in the money I would be able to invest than in my great experience as a publisher, which by now had reached a total of just over four years. Certainly I could not have helped but realize the truth after a luncheon with the one new publisher, now the phenomenally successful promoter of a method of exploiting that excellent commodity, snob appeal, who presented his case very badly and simply. "We're just a year old," he said to me. "I think we've done very well. We've lost only thirty-five thousand in this time, and that's not a bad record, do you think?" I thought it simpler to agree with him at the time. But I did not pursue our negotiations any further.

The actual founding of Covici, Friede came about in a very strange way. In the spring of 1926 Boni & Liveright had published a new book by Heywood Broun. It was a picturesque novel called *Gandle Follows His Nose*, and it called for something very special in the way of exploitation. We hit upon the idea of a contest with a five-hundred-dollar prize for the best picture of Bunny Gandle the hero of the book. The contest drew a lot of good publicity and a mass of very bad pictures. I was one of the judges of the contest, and I went through the submissions with increasing despair. And then I found the picture we had hoped for, a startling black and white signed by a name I had never heard before, Alexander King. When the judges met for the final vote there was no hesitation in reaching a decision. King's picture got our unanimous vote.

When King came to see me at my office to collect his check, he brought with him some drawings he wanted to show me with the vague idea of getting a book to illustrate. It was at the height of the vogue for the Masereel woodcuts, and he had carried this artist's cold disdain for human beings one simple step further. King seemed to hate everything and everybody, and all decent feelings were his very special target. His masterpiece was a black-and-white drawing of a blowzy and pendulous and obviously diseased whore standing stripped in front of an equally obviously drunken sailor, with a sullen madam in the doorway. This charming little item, which hung in my bedroom for a number of years, was entitled *"The Rent's Past Due, Hon,"* and it was greatly admired by my *avant-garde* friends. There were many others, all similar in their approach to things, and I went for them hook, line, and sinker. I tried to interest Liveright in giving King a book to illustrate, but his reaction came as a great disappointment to me. He simply did not like them, and he said so, definitely.

I had, however, made up my mind. Here was my chance to do something for a deserving artist, and I went all out in my efforts on his behalf. I took over our reception room for a three-day exhibit, with a huge party for the opening night of the show. I covered the walls of the room in black cloth and moved the grand piano into another office, where

77

it effectively interfered with any possibility of anybody's getting any work done. I had electricians come in to install the proper lighting, and I had a catalog printed, and invitations too, and sent them to all the art critics and to all our authors and friends. But that was not enough. I took the ten most startling black and whites and had line cuts made of them. I had a thousand sets of these illustrations printed, and I wrote an introduction for a specially designed slip-case folder, with an eleventh drawing on the cover. And I persuaded Liveright to urge his friend Otto Kahn to come to the *vernissage*.

This last step was an essential part of any exhibit in those days. Otto Kahn was the most liberal of philanthropists, both in his ideas and his open-handed generosity, and his approval was worth not only money in the bank but also a form of snobbish prestige second only in value to recognition by Frank Crowninshield and *Vanity Fair*. I went to him often and for the most varied group of struggling young artists imaginable, and never once did he turn me down, even though many of the artists for whom I was bespeaking assistance interested him, I am certain, not at all. I had no idea how he would react to King's work, but I felt that it was important that he be there on the opening night of the showing.

As a party the evening turned out to be a huge success. There was plenty to drink, and there were enough celebrities to satisfy the Leonard Lyonses of that day. And Otto Kahn came and, dutifully, bought. But that was all. There were no other sales, and what was much more important, there were no notices in the papers. I could not understand this at first, and I was very much upset by it. I proceeded to make inquiries, suspecting some sort of conspiracy. And it was then that I discovered an elemental fact that had never occurred to me. Of what use would it be, said the art critics, to run a review of the show if by the time it appeared, the show would no longer be there? They had better use for their space than to run notices for the record only. There was no answer to this. We needed our reception room for the purpose for which it was intended, and even if we could have subjected our writers to many more days of waiting in a room hung solidly in black cloth, garishly lighted with the makeshift equipment we had managed to secure, and dominated by a group of the most depressing pictures ever assembled in one room, it would still have been too late to have done anything about getting the reviews that would have been the only justification for this move. The exhibit closed on schedule, the black cloth came down, and we became a publishing house once again.

But I had made up my mind to sell King, and I have always been a pretty good salesman. It took a lot of work on my part, but I finally succeeded. The Boni & Liveright catalog for the spring of 1927 was embellished with a series of vignettes by King, one for each of the titles in the catalog; King's caricature of Liveright was used by Waldo Frank for his *New Yorker* profile of Liveright; the Sunday *World* ran a weekly dramatic caricature by him on the front page of their magazine section, which was at that time the great repository for all the wits and talents of the period; and Eugene O'Neill agreed to let us bring out a series of limited editions of his plays illustrated by King.

I was greatly helped in my campaign on his behalf by King himself, probably the greatest salesman I have ever known. That he was also one of the greatest storytellers I have ever known—and I mean this in every sense of the word—did not do any harm. I have heard him tell the story of his youth and childhood a dozen times or more, and never, even in two consecutive tellings, has there been one repetition of fact or locale or even of dates. But it never seemed to matter somehow. The story, no matter which version he chose to tell, was always wonderful. He had an absolute genius for holding his audience. I have always been sorry that I could not be in New York when many years after our first meeting he hired a theater and invited all the critics to come and hear him read—and undoubtedly also act out—his new play. He must have been in his glory then.

In any case it was King who first suggested that Covici and I get together. I had met Pat Covici a number of times on his numerous trips to New York, where he tried in every way imaginable to overcome the very real handicap of publishing books in Chicago, a thousand long miles away from the real center of publishing. I had always liked the things he published, lush and unusual books, beautifully if extravagantly printed, and illustrated as no other books were then being illustrated. I had copies of most of his books in my library. They were musts for limited-editions collectors.

I had also always liked Covici. This flamboyant Roumanian with the shock of white hair on a poet's head, which in turn was set on a football player's six-foot-three body, was, is, and always will be one of the most unusual men I have ever known. We were to be associated in business for the next ten years, and almost as closely in many other ways after that, and in all that time we never once fought or had any real basic disagreement. Very probably the reason for this could be found in one of Covici's many quotations from his Roumanian grandfather. "When two people tell you you're drunk," Covici would quote him as saying, "go to bed." It was applied by him to any and all differences of opinion. And he followed his own advice and expected the people who worked with him to follow it too. The result was an effectively harmonious relationship that made life enjoyable and exciting.

Not that he was easily swayed. He was a fighter, and

bitterly stubborn about the things he believed in. He had courageously published Ben Hecht's *Fantasius Malare*, with its superphallic illustrations by Wallace Smith, a few years before, and when the postal authorities had stepped in and arrested them all, it had been Covici who had held out longest for a court fight to test the case. He never got over the fact that he finally agreed to plead *nolo contendere* and paid a thousand-dollar fine, as did the other two. He did not believe in censorship of any kind, and that was that.

I had never seen the bookshop that he ran for so long in Chicago and that had led him into publishing. But I had heard a great deal about it, and about the unusual books and equally unusual people he collected in it. It was already firmly part of the Midwest legend. So also was that strange weekly the *Chicago Literary Times*, which Ben Hecht and Charles MacArthur and Maxwell Bodenheim and all the others of the Chicago Group published under his auspices. But the *Times* was no more, and neither was the bookshop, and Hecht and MacArthur and Bodenheim and Harry Hansen had all come to New York and were rapidly taking root there. The time had come for a move, and Covici knew it. He responded as eagerly as I did to King's suggestion that we get together.

In deference to King's function as the entrepreneur, we met at his house for dinner the night Covici arrived from Chicago. With only occasional interruptions we continued our talks for the next three days. At the end of that time we were in basic agreement on almost all points, and most certainly on the main one of wanting to publish books together. A new publishing house was in the process of being born.

And now my brother got the auditors back on the job, and they went to Chicago to check up on the financial value of Pascal Covici, Inc., Publisher. They finally established the book value of that firm at the sum of thirty thousand dollars. That was to be Covici's contribution to the new firm. Mine was thirty thousand dollars in cash, a good part of what remained of my once large inheritance. But that did not worry me much. The trust fund would build itself up again as Liveright's monthly checks came in. And I was certain that Covici, Friede would make a lot of money for us both.

So for the next two months Covici and I smiled politely as our lawyers and auditors battled out their differences. It seemed like a pretty silly performance to both of us, but if things had to be done that way, we had to make the best of it. Only we wished that they would hurry up and give us the necessary papers to sign so that we could get ourselves incorporated, staffed, installed—and into our first list. The fall of 1929 was to see the first publications under our joint imprint. And there was plenty of work yet to be done. Excepting for three limited editions we hoped would be ready in time for fall publication, two of which were to be illustrated by Alexander King, we had by mid-April very little idea of what we were going to publish four months later.

And we certainly had no idea that almost exactly one year later we would be drawing a check for sixty-four thousand dollars, slightly in excess of our total capitalization, to the order of Radclyffe Hall—an author whose existence we did not even suspect at this time—as her first royalty check on *The Well of Loneliness*.

SEVEN

THE
BOY
GROWS
UP

THE first offices of Covici, Friede were in a run-of-the-mill office building on West Forty-fifth Street. Seven-foot-high partitions—it took me five years to persuade Covici that private offices with doors did not mean that everybody would automatically soldier on the job—broke up our rather limited floor space into a reasonable facsimile of private and outer offices. Our shipping room and a good part of our stock took up almost half of our floor space. But actually it did not matter too much. Our entire staff consisted of seven people, including Covici and myself, and there was plenty of room for us.

Covici and I divided the selling, manufacturing, advertising, and publicity jobs between us, on a vaguely communal basis. His wife Dorothy was the business department while my wife was the editorial department. There was one shipping clerk who had come on from Chicago with the Covicis, and who lived with them at first until he got homesick three months later and went back West. There was one stenographer, and there was one girl who took

83

dictation when she was not occupied at either the switchboard or at one of the very elaborate billing machines we installed almost at once.

That was our organization when we began publishing. It was quite sufficient for our purposes, for we had started our house at the apex of the limited-edition craze, and the selling of limited editions by a publisher, with good taste in content, typography, and illustrations, plus a good mailing list, was not the most difficult of problems in the summer and fall of 1928. By sacrificing taste in content, and often in illustrations as well, even better results could be obtained. Polite erotica, in editions of five to fifteen hundred copies, at prices ranging from ten to twenty-five dollars, never stayed on the booksellers' shelves very long. They were the twentieth-century version of the library set, except that they were usually sold by means of very elaborate circulars, rather than by house-to-house canvassers. Covici had brought the art of limited-edition publishing to a high state in Chicago. Together we proceeded to improve it still further.

Our first publications, even before we got around to issuing our first catalog, were two limited editions—a new translation of Villon with illustrations by Alexander King, of which we printed nine hundred and sixty sets at twenty dollars the set; and a run of one hundred copies only of *The Gospel of the Goat*, a thirty-two page book of lithographs by Alexander King, for which we asked twenty-two fifty a copy. There was also one regular trade book, *The Sweet Singer of Michigan*, by Mrs. Julia Moore, a reprint of probably the worst volume of poetry ever written by anybody, anywhere. It was of this book that Frank Sullivan wrote his classic line, "Don't miss it if you can."

With these books out of the way, we sat down to try to plan our first real list. Ben Hecht and Charles MacArthur had just finished a play, *The Front Page*, and it was about to be tried out on the road. Since Covici and I between us had published almost everything that Hecht had ever written, it was only natural for us to want to publish his first play. We had no idea, of course, of how it would go on Broadway, and we had no illusions about its possible sales in book form. Published plays did not sell then, and the very sedate *New York Times* did not review them in its book section. But Hecht was a good name, and we needed names badly. It was a very pleasant surprise to all of us when the play became both a smash hit and the first published version of an American play to sell in any appreciable quantity.

We soon had a few more books lined up, a so-called sequel to *The Three Musketeers* by the indefatigable H. Bedford-Jones, a fine narrative poem about a Negro prize fighter by Joseph Moncure March, a book of short stories by a Russian scientist with an introduction by Theodore Dreiser that guaranteed the sale of one copy to every collector of Dreiser first editions, a couple of first novels that seemed to us very promising, and the *Collected Poems* by Richard Aldington. The rest of our list was pure wishful thinking, and more limited editions, with illustrations by Majeska, the very exotic-minded daughter of a conservative Philadelphia family, Jean de Bosschere—and Alexander King.

We knew that this list would make money for us, but we wanted more than that. We were literary adventurers, and the idea of buying established authors away from their publishers did not appeal to us very much. What we wanted to do was to discover new writers and build them up. With the backlog of limited editions we were acquiring —we commissioned a new translation of the *Canterbury Tales* and laid out a very ambitious five-volume project, the Lawn Bank Keats, which was to be a complete edition of all his works together with all his letters, and which would sell for seventy-five dollars—we felt we could afford this very chancy method of publishing. But where to find these writers in short order?

Covici and I were discussing this problem in my office one day. We had just signed a contract for a novel with one of the more promising *transition* authors, and that led us naturally into a survey of the *avant-garde* group, and as naturally to a discussion of Wyndham Lewis, the English writer who, despairing of finding any other artists as radical as himself, had set himself up as a one-man movement. We both admired his writings, and we discussed the advisability of writing to London to ask him about his plans. We were just about to draft our letter to him when the phone rang. Covici answered it, and I thought he looked somewhat startled when he hung up the phone after telling the operator to send him in. He shook his head in disbelief when he turned back to me. "Wyndham Lewis," he said. "In the outside office. He wants to talk to us."

The inevitable result was that we agreed to publish the first part of a three-part Joycean novel Lewis was completing. We could not have done otherwise: it would have been tempting the fates. When we saw our sales figures on volume one, we began to wish we had tempted them. And when the question of undertaking volumes two and three came up, we decided that, fates or no fates, we must risk turning these books down. After all, we were not publishing for the sole purpose of building an ever plentiful stockroom.

We added a few more books in the next weeks, and our first list began to have some meaning as well as the necessary bulk. But we still lacked two things without which we felt we could not consider ourselves real publishers, a detective story and a game book. We decided to combine them both in one volume, to be called very simply *Murder*, which would consist of some thirty-six short descriptions of crimes with all the clues there for the average reader and with the solutions in a sealed envelope at the back of the book. The fact that this book existed only in our minds, and that we wanted to publish it in the early fall, did not bother us at all. My wife and I had had the idea for some time, and we had often discussed it with an aspiring young writer friend of ours, Gretta Palmer, the wife of the Sunday-magazine editor of the *New York World*. Gretta moved out to our house in Larchmont, and in less than a month she and my wife wrote over fifty short crime stories from which we picked the best ones, edited and polished them, and sent the manuscript to the printer.

It was obvious that this book needed some very special type of promotion, and we decided to make sure that it got it. Skywriting was in its infancy at the time, and we decided that the word "murder" in mile-high letters all over the sky was exactly what we needed. We had no difficulty in making a deal with the only fliers who were then operating skywriting planes. They were just as anxious as we were to see what the results would be, and they agreed to spell the word out for six solid days on the understanding that they would receive ten cents per copy for every copy sold during that period. We on our part agreed to run advertisements in the papers during this week, explaining to the bewildered New Yorkers why, as we put it, "Murder is in the air," and urging them to run, not walk, to the nearest bookstore for their copy of the book. It seemed like a wonderful stunt, and we could not see how it could miss.

But miss it did, and dismally. The trouble was that all of us, including the skywriters, had made absolutely no allowance for weather conditions. And for three solid weeks after publication there was not one day clear enough for skywriting. If it was not raining it was either too cloudy or too windy, and in the meantime the bookstores, who had been most co-operative, had huge piles of the book in stock with not one line of advertising having appeared in any of the papers. And when the weather finally cleared, it did so only in spurts and on very short notice. The result was that the six days agreed upon were spread over a period of almost a month, and never once did we manage to place our ads in relation to a day in which the planes went up, spelling the completely mystifying word "murder" in the sky for no apparent purpose.

Only the fact that we managed to sell the second serial rights to the book to a news syndicate kept us from taking a really large loss. But the poor skywriters, having lived up to their part of the contract, did not fare as well. They knew how complete the fiasco had been, and they never bothered to get in touch with us to collect their share of the sales of the book. It was good that they didn't: it wouldn't even have paid for the gasoline they used.

There was one other book Covici urged us to add to our list. It was a novel called *O Lost* that he had read in Chicago. The beauty of its prose had excited the poet in him, but he had not been geared for trade publishing at the time. One of the first things he did when he got to New York was to ask the agent who had sent it to him there to let us see it. A messenger boy brought it to us, staggering under the weight of two huge bundles of manuscript, and I, appalled at the size of the book, turned it over to the editorial department. I got the report a few days later, and it did not excite me too much. It was very short and to the point, and it read as follows: "A semi-autobiographical novel of well over 500,000 words, relating the history of a family over a period of 50 years. It is fearfully diffuse, and it would be a tremendous piece of work to boil it down. In parts it holds one's interest by its vitality, but it is marred by stylistic cliches, outlandish adjectives and similes, etc. Probably the author could write if he dumped this overboard and began again. I do not believe it would be possible or worth while to doctor this up. It has all the faults of youth and inexperience."

I showed the report to Covici. He shook his head sadly. Yes, he admitted, he was afraid that that was what would happen. It did, he admitted, need radical cutting. Maybe if we had the author in and spoke to him— We laughed. No need to bother him, we said. The report made it very clear that it was and would remain unpublishable, whatever cutting and editing might be done. Another messenger boy staggered back to the agent with the manuscript.

Even now, many years later, I still feel that we were right in turning down the book, something, incidentally, that had been done by some twenty other publishers. The fact that it was accepted by Scribner's, retitled *Look Homeward, Angel*, and made Thomas Wolfe a major writer overnight cannot alter the fact that the manuscript we saw bore little relation to the book that finally appeared. That book was the product of the genius of one of the greatest editors I have ever known, Maxwell Perkins of Scribner's. Without him *Look Homeward, Angel*, would ever have remained *O Lost*, making its weary way from publisher to publisher.

We did very well with our first list. It was an exciting experience to see my name on a book, and it was exciting to see the orders and reorders coming in. It was fun to wear the black Borsalino hats that Hecht gave each of us after the opening of *The Front Page*, and fun to watch the next list take shape. Altogether those first few months were a heady period.

But they were as nothing compared to what we had in store for us. I was in the habit of going up to Dreiser's country home, just outside of Pleasantville, to sit in the aerie he had built himself there and to enjoy the strange assortment of people with whom he surrounded himself.

I also went there to enjoy Dreiser himself. In that I was perhaps unique. His cantankerousness was notorious, and it is a definite fact that at some time or other in his life he managed to quarrel with almost everyone he had ever known. And some of these arguments turned into lasting enmities.

But I will always be very proud of the fact that in all the years I knew Dreiser we never had even the slightest of disagreements. As his publisher, as the self-appointed scapegoat in the Boston trial of *An American Tragedy*, and later as his motion-picture agent, my relationship with him was always warm and exciting. I loved the old man, and I loved to sit at his feet and listen to him probing and questing and searching out the innermost recesses of the minds of those about him. His curiosity was insatiable. He had to know everything there was to be known, and on every imaginable subject. He did a pretty good job of it too.

In any case it was at Pleasantville that I heard some news about a new novel which had just been published by Jonathan Cape in England, and had been suppressed overnight. A contract for an American edition had been signed with Knopf, and the book had been set up by him so that publication could take place in time to protect the copyright. Now it was rumored that Knopf did not care to chance the publication of this book and had so notified Cape. I came back from Dreiser's in a state of high excitement. From everything everybody there said about the book—it was by a woman named Radclyffe Hall and dealt with the taboo subject of Lesbianism—it was a fine and sincere piece of writing, and besides it carried the endorsement of Havelock Ellis, which certainly precluded the possibility of its being merely another bit of pornography. I made up my mind to get it.

But how were we to go about doing this? It was not an

easy problem. Other publishers had the same idea, and it was obvious that there would be a bidding race. A cable to Cape offering to publish the book and to pay the legal cost should there be an attempt to suppress it here drew a flat no from him. So did a series of cables in which we gradually increased our offer to include a progressively larger advance against a straight fifteen-per-cent royalty. It began to look as if we would not get the book after all.

That was the state of affairs when I sat in Macy's one day, waiting to see the buyer with some of our fall publications. And it was there I was told two things. A major publisher had offered seventy-five hundred dollars advance to Cape, half again as much as we had. And Cape had sailed for America the previous day. Suddenly I knew exactly what we had to do to get the book. Forgetting all about my appointment with the Macy buyer, I dashed back to the office.

I told Covici what I wanted to do. We would wireless Cape to the steamer offering a ten-thousand-dollar advance against a straight twenty-per-cent royalty. Moreover the advance would be nonreturnable in case we were not permitted to publish the book. And we would hire an attorney at once, and instead of giving him a flat fee, we would, in exchange for his services, pay him twenty-five cents for every copy of the book we sold in America. And all this would be made possible by the fact that we would publish the book at five dollars rather than the conventional two fifty. I was convinced that we would have no trouble getting this much for it.

Covici listened to me carefully, nodding agreement to every point. The idea, he admitted, was excellent in all its details. And such an offer would probably result in our getting the book. But where, he asked me, did I propose to get the ten thousand dollars? Surely, he said, I must know that we could not possibly draw a check for that amount of money for any purpose, and for the very simple reason that we did not have anything like that sum in the bank. We had just finished shipping our first list, he reminded me, the booksellers were just beginning to pay for the books they had ordered, and besides we had already used a good part of our limited cash resources for advances on other books. Or was it maybe that I proposed to lend the firm the ten thousand dollars?

I shook my head. Not at all, I said. I couldn't imagine my brother or my mother agreeing to let me withdraw still another large sum from my trust fund, and for the special purpose of publishing a book that had been suppressed in England and might be suppressed here too. I proposed to get it, I said, from our bank, from the very conservative president of the very conservative Fifth Avenue Bank. If Covici was willing I would go to see him at once and tell him exactly why we wanted the money. I was convinced that we would get it.

And that is exactly what happened. I pulled no punches at the bank. I admitted frankly that the book had been suppressed in England and that it might meet the same fate here. And if it did, then we might never have the opportunity of earning the advance we had paid Radclyffe Hall. And that money, plus our entire investment in the manufacturing of the book, would be a dead loss. But, I added, I thought we had more than an even chance of winning our case here. And if we did, there was no limit to what our sales could be. Seated back of his old-fashioned roll-top oak desk in the open offices of the bank, the president listened to me carefully and then nodded. "Go ahead," he said. "Make the offer. If it is accepted, you can have the money."

The wireless went out to Cape within the hour. Late that afternoon we got our answer. Obviously the offer was much too good to turn down: Cape accepted.

The contracts were signed a few days after Cape landed. But there was one last-minute hitch. When he came to the usual option clause, which gave us first call on Radclyffe Hall's next two books, Cape shook his head. "I'm afraid," he said, "that I can't give you that option." We made no objection to his crossing out this paragraph. Obviously, we said to ourselves, Cape is only acting for the author in connection with this one book. There will be time enough to discuss it with her when I see her in Europe in the spring. If we've done a good job for her, there will be no trouble in getting her next books.

What we did not know was that Cape's trip to America was only secondarily for the purpose of making *The Well of Loneliness* deal. His primary purpose was to sign the final papers with Harrison Smith for the establishment of his American house. It had been his hope to publish *The Well of Loneliness* himself, and only the fact that if he had waited until his house was functioning, he might have jeopardized the copyright of the book had finally made him accept our offer. But he had no intention of giving up the publication rights to Radclyffe Hall's next books, the option for which was very definitely included in his contract with her. A semanticist could have objected to his use of the word "can't," but it was not a dishonest use. It was merely a question of his outsmarting us. And besides, "semantics" was a word none of us had ever heard at that time.

With the contract signed and the money passed, we went to see Morris Ernst, whose book on censorship, *To the Pure*, was on the Viking fall list. He was happy to make the deal we suggested. Not only did it promise to be very profitable, but it would be excellent publicity for his book. He laid out a detailed plan, which we agreed to follow. And his first suggestion was that we include the Havelock Ellis quote as part of the published book. In that way we could be sure that it would have to be used in evidence.

The next step was to take over the plates of the book from Knopf. And it was then that we made another discovery. Knopf had already printed a sizable number of copies so as to be certain of being able to protect the copyright, and it became necessary for us to take the sheets of these books over from him too. And since Knopf quite rightly added all his charges in connection with the proposed publication of the book to his cost sheet on the copies he had already printed, the result was that we faced a loss on these copies even if we sold them at five dollars. We solved this problem very simply. Knopf had used a very fine paper on his edition, and we merely printed a new title page, numbered all the copies, called it a pre-publication limited edition, and sold out the entire edition overnight at ten dollars a copy.

Our sales of the regular edition were tremendous, and our profits huge. And when John S. Sumner stepped in and haled us into court, sales doubled overnight. In order to keep on publishing the book we had some time before taken the precaution of moving our plates from New York to a manufacturing plant in New Jersey, and we kept on shipping from there until the upper courts finally decided in our favor. And even when that had happened the book continued to sell. That was something we had not expected. In fact we had been so doubtful on this point that I had made a special trip to Boston to see if the Watch and Ward Society could not be tricked into taking action on the book. I have always thought I was subtle in my approach to them, but evidently I still had much to learn. In any case they assured me that they saw nothing wrong with the book, even though, as I pointed out to them, both England and New York had suppressed it. We could continue to sell it in Boston, they announced, without any danger of any move on their part. This was very definitely not what I wanted to hear, but I had to be satisfied with it.

Thanks to *The Well of Loneliness* we were off to a roaring start. Our limited editions were selling beautifully too, and we were tying up all our large profits, and a good part of our capital as well, in fees for new translations, and typographical plans and illustrations. We signed a contract with Rockwell Kent for our *Canterbury Tales*, and we increased our commitment with Jean de Bosschere from one to two books a year. And then I went to Europe to add new illustrators to our list.

In Paris I made the rounds of the artists' studios. I went to see Foujita in his lushly Oriental home, and tried not to be too much aware of his bangs and Harold Lloyd glasses and earrings as I made arrangements for him to do a book of twenty lithographs of cats for us. I called on Colette in an apartment so overheated and so overfilled with knick-knacks that I could neither breathe nor move, and tried to get her to do the text for the Foujita book. But she wanted so much money for the few words she would have written that I was forced to leave this perfect marriage unconsummated. I did get Helene Perdriat to agree to do illustrations for *Madame Bovary*, and I talked to a number of other painters about various schemes we had in mind. Taken all in all, however, the trip was not a terrific success —except for one thing.

I had looked up Richard Aldington as soon as I had arrived. I had expected to find him scholarly and dry. Instead I found a young and eager drinking companion who introduced me to the Bateau Ivre, the night club where I spent most of my evenings while I was in Paris. Covici had been publishing Aldington for years, both his poetry and his truly fine translations. At one time, as a matter of fact, Aldington's weekly remittance from Covici exceeded the small sum Covici permitted himself to draw from his Chicago publishing house. One of the very first questions I asked Aldington was if he had ever thought about writing any fiction. Why yes, he said, he had. Some years back he had started a novel. But he put it aside and had never finished it. Could I see it? I asked. Certainly, he said, he'd send over the few chapters he had written. And he'd be interested in hearing what I thought of them.

I took the Dunkerque-Tillbury boat for England that night, and comfortably propped up in my cabin, with a drunken troupe of midgets carousing in the corridors, I read the hundred-odd pages of manuscript Aldington had sent me. I cannot remember when any manuscript has ever moved me more. I wired Aldington as soon as I got to London. He was to drop everything else, I said, in order to finish the novel. We would see to it that he would have enough money to make this possible. And then I cabled Covici and told him to add Aldington's first novel to our fall list. The title of it, I told him, was *Death of a Hero*, and it was the finest war novel I had ever read. I reread it just a few months ago and I still feel that way about it.

From London I flew to Berlin. I had a wild idea about getting Albert Einstein to write his autobiography, and I felt that the best way to go about getting it was to see him and talk to him about it. I introduced myself to Mrs. Einstein over the phone, explained my mission, and made an appointment for early in the afternoon. I was under the impression that the professor would be present, but when I arrived at the dark and massive apartment, so typically and heavily German, where they lived, I discovered that I was to be disappointed. Frau Einstein was very polite and very firm. Professor Einstein was a scientist. He was not interested in invading other fields. He could not entertain my proposals. He hoped I had not made this long trip for the sole purpose of talking to him. He was sorry that he would be unable to see me.

Actually my trip to Germany had been made with this one visit in mind. But since I was there anyway, I decided to see if I could not salvage something out of the wreckage. I called on a number of the publishers in Berlin and Leipzig, trying to find some books that might lend themselves to American publication. But the minute I spotted a title that looked promising I came up against one of two regretful answers. "So sorry," the publisher would say, "but Herr Knopf has the option on this book." And if it was not Herr Knopf, then it would be Herr Huebsch of the Viking Press who had got there first. It seemed as if they had parceled out all German literature between them. I had to be satisfied with two books, both of which cost a great deal of money, and neither of which ever even came close to earning the advances I agreed to pay. It would have been much more profitable for me to have left Germany immediately after my abortive non-interview with Einstein.

I came back to Paris to make the final arrangements with Aldington about *Death of a Hero* and to sit on the balcony of Radclyffe Hall's apartment watching the impressive spectacle of Foch's funeral and marveling at the sight of the Prince of Wales, complete in a huge shako, which still left him shorter by inches than Pershing beside whom he marched in the funeral procession. And then I sailed for New York.

Back there I found that our offices were rapidly becoming a madhouse. Intoxicated by the success of *The Well of Loneliness* and by the continuing sales of our limited editions, we were expanding like mad. Joseph Margolies, the book buyer at Brentano's, had come in with us as sales manager. George Joel, who had been handling publicity for the Brentano publishing ventures, became our publicity man. And our small offices bulged with assistant editors and foreign editors, and billing clerks and typists. Even tearing out our shipping room and moving it into separate offices across the hall did not help very much. We began to look around for new quarters. It was obvious that we would need them.

Our fall list was as usual half limited editions. As a matter of fact we issued a special and very elaborate catalog of these books, with a foreword by Vincent Starrett, thereby making the catalog itself a collector's item. The leading title on this list was our new translation, into what we called "racy contemporary American idiom," of the complete works of Rabelais. Covici had commissioned Samuel Putnam to do the job while he was still publishing in Chicago, and Putnam had been living in France for a number of years, devoting himself to the tremendous task he had undertaken. As a piece of bookmaking too the undertaking was colossal. The edition ran to 1,338 pages, 10 by 13 in size, with the copious notes printed on the margins of the pages to which they referred. There were two editions announced. One, at fifty dollars and optimistically limited to thirteen hundred sets, featured twenty-four illustrations, in all the colors of the rainbow plus a lavish use of gold leaf, by Jean de Bosschere. The other, austerely limited to only two hundred sets, which were offered at one hundred and thirty-five dollars the set, contained eighty illustrations by Alexander King. In addition both editions included one hundred and twenty drawings, which we cautiously labeled as being "attributed" to Rabelais.

But even in those free and easy days, when anybody could sell anything for any price, we came close to coming a cropper on this book. We had planned it for three volumes, bulked as all limited editions were bulked then, and solidly boxed in cardboard. But the books, when they finally reached us from the binders, weighed a total of fully twenty-five pounds, and no cardboard known to man could contain them without breaking. That was bad enough, but it was only part of the sad story. The worst thing about this edition was that, for some reason we could

never understand, the designer of the edition had not divided it into three equal volumes of four hundred-odd
pages each. Instead, the first volume ran to well over six
hundred pages and weighed almost fifteen pounds, while
the other two volumes ran to four hundred and three hundred pages respectively. It was a physical impossibility to
hold the first volume, let alone read it, and the booksellers
threw up their hands in horror when they saw it. Somehow we managed to sell about half of each of the editions,
and then we quickly got rid of the sets we were still stuck
with, at ten dollars the set, to the leading mail-order dealers
in polite erotica, a firm that called itself the American
Anthropological Society. They sold their copies quickly
and at a good profit. But we did not begrudge them anything they made. Thanks to them we almost managed to
break even on the venture.

Our regular list was pretty exciting. We had, in addition to Aldington's *Death of a Hero*, a fine novel by Fran-
çois Mauriac; *Wings Over Europe*, the Theatre Guild play
by Robert Nichols that managed to anticipate the atom
bomb by fifteen years and proposed a solution for it that
the world might have done well to heed; and a novel
translated from the Russian of a Parisian refugee from
Soviet Russia, a talented and promising young writer
named Ilya Ehrenburg. There was also on this list probably the plushest book ever published. It was the autobiography of a young colored singer, Taylor Gordon, who
had started his career singing in a Montana bordello. It
was naïvely and entertainingly written, but it obviously
needed some kind of window dressing to make it sell. It
got it from us, and in full measure. When the book was
published it carried an introduction by Muriel Draper, a
foreword by Carl Van Vechten, and illustrations in color
by Covarrubias. It made a perfect remainder a few seasons
later.

There was one other mishap in connection with that 1929 fall list. I had arranged to have Foujita's lithographs reproduced in Paris under his personal supervision. He was to sign one of the lithographs for each of the five hundred and fifty copies of the edition, and he was also to sign and number the book itself. One day early in the fall we were notified by the customs authorities that the material had arrived from Paris, and we made immediate arrangements to have the reproductions delivered to our binders. But when we went to look at them we made a startling discovery: not one of the lithographs was signed, and the special limit page, handsomely set up and beautifully printed, was also completely devoid both of signature and of numbers. We cabled to Paris at once and received a most apologetic answer. It was regrettable, we were informed, there had been a slight mistake. If we would return the material to be signed they would see to it that Monsieur Foujita did so at once. We had five hundred and fifty lithographs and an equal number of limit pages packed at top speed and sent back to Paris on the next steamer. And two days after the boat had sailed we received a letter from Foujita. He had been called to Japan unexpectedly, he wrote. He hoped it would not inconvenience us too much to have the material he was to sign sent on to Japan. He would take care of things as soon as the lithographs reached him, and would see to it that they were immediately returned to us. Actually it was almost a year later before we saw them again, and when they did finally arrive, miraculously undamaged after traveling one and a half times around the world, the depression had started and a limited edition of lithographs of cats at twenty-five dollars the copy was almost as unsalable as a street corner apple at a dime. But they did make fine presents, and for years our friends, whether they loved or hated cats, would be solemnly presented with gifts of beautifully framed Foujitas:

I gave my last one away only a few months ago.

But we had no thought of a depression in the early fall of 1929. The market was still climbing, and most of us were in it, as were our barbers and our bootblacks and our elevator men. Our problem was to find space enough for all the employees we had managed to acquire, and to get offices that would better suit our new station in the publishing world. The previous year, when we had started our firm so blithely, we had never known from season to season where our next list was coming from. Now we had enough limited editions planned and contracted for to take care of our problems in that direction for many years to come. We had ploughed back all the money we had made on our first lists of limited editions, as well as most of the money we had made on *The Well of Loneliness*, into advances to artists and editors and typographers and translators. And we had managed to build up a fairly good list of writers too, authors from whom we could expect new and salable books yearly. Now we had to move. Our offices were quickly becoming as crowded as the Marx Brothers' cabin.

We took space in a fine building on Fourth Avenue, in the center of the publishing district of that day. Perhaps the fact that I had just moved to East Tenth Street, and that the offices were therefore less than a mile from my home, had something to do with our making the choice we did. In any case we moved in the early fall, and this time I managed to persuade Covici that there should be three private offices, complete with walls. But the others were still only spaces surrounded with seven-foot partitions. And Covici's own office, the door to which was rarely closed, was so situated that he could see everything that was going on.

Less than three months after we moved, the market cracked, and the boom years ended. And as we came into the beginnings of the depression we had close to two hundred thousand dollars tied up in limited editions, most of which were still in such early stages of their planning that their major costs still lay ahead of us.

EIGHT

JUST
AROUND
THE
CORNER

*T*o THE great optimist in the White House in the fall of 1929 the thing to be found around that mythical and never-to-be-reached corner was, of course, prosperity. To us it came to mean creditors: worried creditors, impatient creditors, demanding creditors—in fact every kind of creditor except a satisfied one. And yet, somehow or other, we kept going for eight more years, and we managed to publish some good books in those years, and to publish them well. And when the end finally came we were just a few months short of publishing what would have been the most successful book we had ever undertaken, John Steinbeck's *The Grapes of Wrath*.

Of course our immediate problem was not quite so bad as the one that faced the very new firm of Farrar and Rinehart. They had put on a really terrific campaign for a game book that they expected would sweep the country. It was called *Speculation—The Game of Wall Street*, and all the windows of all the bookstores in the financial district were filled with copies of the book on publication day, October

21—exactly three days before the market cracked wide open and Richard Whitney made his dramatic and futile attempt to keep United States Steel from dropping below 200. I have often wondered what became of all these books. After the happenings on that day they were not even good drugstore-counter fodder.

We had no book as topical as this one, and therefore we could take the universally optimistic view that all these unfortunate happenings were merely temporary and that very soon now stocks would start climbing again, people would have money to spend, and all would be well in this best of possible worlds. There were a few adjustments that had to be made by those of us who had done too much pyramiding of paper profits—my brother, in Europe when the crash came, had had the brilliant idea of going for a long cross-country drive immediately after he got the first word of the crash, convinced that if his brokers could not get in touch with him with their desperate cables asking for additional margin, they would not think of selling him out—but since in most cases our original investments had been fairly small, the adjustments were not too difficult to make. And for the next year the book business continued to be good, probably because people found that they could get a good deal of enjoyment out of actually reading the books they had become accustomed to buying so lavishly.

In 1930 we were really beginning to hit our stride as publishers. We still depended on our limited editions for our profit, but our regular list was beginning to look and feel more balanced. There were new novels by Aldington and Mauriac and Fulton Oursler. There was Margaret Anderson's delightful story of the *Little Review*, *My Thirty Years' War*, and two books by E. E. Cummings that defied classification, and new volumes of verse by Horace Gregory and Aldington. And there was also our first detective story, which definitely established us as publishers—we had passed the semifinal test when we published a cook book, a very rococo affair called *The Gourmets' Almanac*, the previous year.

The author of this detective story was Fulton Oursler, but since he already appeared on our list as a serious novelist under his own name—his wife, Grace Perkins, wrote for us under two names—he felt he should use a pseudonym for this book. And since he was inventing a name to use, it seemed to him an excellent idea to choose a name beginning with "A." In that way he would head any alphabetical list of writers, with the consequent advantage of coming to the book buyer's attention before he bogged down in the late "R's" or early "S's." He suggested Anthony Abbot, explaining to us carefully that the two "b's" would put him ahead of his only alphabetical competitor, Achmed Abdullah. We were very much impressed, so much so that we made another suggestion to him. Why not, we asked, so word the titles of the books that they too would come at the head of the list alphabetically? For instance, he wanted to call his first detective story *The Murder of Geraldine Foster*. A good title too, we said. But supposing he put the word "About" in front of this title? Wouldn't that make it just a little better? Because then, we pointed out to him, there could be no question of his being at the head of the list, no matter if the list was an author's list or a list of titles. And if it happened to be a combined list, then he'd be there twice, in first and second position. He applauded our acumen, and we all went out and had a drink together.

There was another of our books that, like *The Well of Loneliness*, came to us as a result of a Sunday spent at Dreiser's country house. This was Dr. van de Velde's classic sex book *Ideal Marriage*. It had just been published in London by the very staid firm of Heineman, but in spite of this guarantee of its character, no American publisher, or so T. R. Smith assured me, had dared to consider publishing it. The big barrier, it seemed, was that the book contained a detailed chapter on sexual positions, listing either sixteen or seventeen different ones, T. R. could not remember which. And that sounded much too much like an open invitation for John S. Sumner, the vigilant guardian of New York's morals, to step in and stop publication. I called Covici when I got back to town that night, and we both agreed that it sounded like a book we wanted to publish. We cabled Heineman an offer and got a cabled acceptance.

When we saw the book itself a few weeks later we began to wonder if we had made a mistake. There was the chapter on positions, and it was even more detailed than T. R. had suggested. And there were a lot of other things in the book that looked just as dangerous. But we decided to chance it, and we thought we might as well kill two birds with one stone by pricing it at seven and a half dollars. Nobody could accuse us of trying to corrupt the youth of America with a seven-and-a-half-dollar book—and the profit on a seven-and-a-half-dollar book was three times as large as it would have been had the book been priced at three and a half dollars, which is what its price would have been under normal circumstances. To play absolutely safe we positively restricted its sale to "Physicians, lawyers, ministers, and educators." We were to be very much surprised in the next few years at the number of people who fell into one or more of these categories.

Much to our surprise nobody tried to interfere with our publishing the book. We had been certain that either Sumner or the Watch and Ward Society would make some move, and equally certain that the courts would sustain us in the end. But an afternoon spent with Sumner's assistant on the spurious plea that I was trying to show them why this book was a book of such impeccable standing that they should not try to stop us from publishing it, and two hours spent in the offices of the Watch and Ward Society in Boston for the same purpose, both proved completely fruitless. They all agreed with me completely. There was no doubt at all, they said, but that this was an honest and valuable book, and they both assured me they would do nothing to interfere with us. Even when we dropped the restrictions on its sale, there was still no objection from them. In time the book came to be accepted for the classic it really is, and I like to feel that many people who were denied access to good sexual advice have received it from this book—which continues to sell, still at seven and a half dollars, on the Random House list, having been taken over by the very astute Bennett Cerf when Covici, Friede ceased to exist.

Also on our fall list was a book that we never published, but on which we took a bigger loss than we ever did on any other book, published or unpublished. It was announced as *The Private Papers of Casanova*, and Lewis Galantière was supposed to translate it for us. I forget who first told us about these "lost" papers, but I do know that we all got very excited about getting our hands on them. The transatlantic telephone had just begun to function, and I put in a call to someone in Europe to get on the trail of them at once. A few days later I got a call from him. He had located the papers, he informed me. There were exactly sixty-nine documents written by Casanova in the last fourteen years of his life while he was acting as librarian to Count Joseph Waldstein at the Castle of Dux. He had seen the documents, he said, and they had been definitely authenticated. However, he had not been permitted to examine them closely, and had been definitely refused permission to read them. They would have to be purchased sight unseen, and the price would be six thousand dollars. Go ahead, we said. Buy them at once and get them to us in the next mail. Agreed, he said. Cable me the money and I will close the deal at once.

We waited impatiently to see what we had bought. And while we were waiting we released a story about our forthcoming publication of this material that made most of the papers in the country. We even had inquiries about it from the news syndicates. Would we please let them see it, they asked, as possible feature material? We assured them that we would. We were very proud of ourselves for having pulled off this coup.

But when we finally saw the material we felt quite differently. It was dull, unimportant, completely unpublishable. There was no rhyme or reason in these pieces, no thread that would justify their being put between book covers. They were merely the senile meanderings of a worn-out rake. We put them in our safe and forgot them. I don't remember how we finally disposed of them.

By midsummer of 1930 it became obvious that the whole face of the book business—and of all other businesses as well—was changing, and that we had to do some pretty radical changing ourselves if we wanted to survive. We took stock of ourselves and came to the very unpleasant conclusion that for an unforeseeably long time the market for limited editions was gone. Our mailing lists, which in the past had helped us to dispose of the major part of any limited edition we chose to publish, were now drawing only fractional returns. And the bookstores were ordering sparingly if at all. Yet we had well over three times our original capitalization tied up in advances and preliminary costs on this type of publication. We thought it over carefully, took a deep breath, and then wrote off every penny we had invested in future limited editions. Illustrations, translations, typographical plans, all of them paid for in full, went into the safe until times should improve. They never did. The safe was still bulging when we ceased to exist eight years later.

There was one limited edition, however, that we could

not put away for storage. This was the translation into modern English verse of *The Canterbury Tales*, for which Rockwell Kent had produced more than fifty illustrations. This two-volume folio job was already completely set up in type, and plates for the two-color illustrations had all been made. We decided that we might as well take a chance on it. We were in too deep to back out now.

It had been our plan to issue fourteen hundred and fifty sets of this edition at fifty dollars the set. We had also planned to offer fifty sets at two hundred and fifty dollars. These special copies—a limited limited edition, so to speak —were to be bound in pigskin, and featured an extra run of the illustrations, printed in continuous panels of five, each panel signed by Kent. For a while we thought of eliminating this de luxe edition, but this would have thrown our production-cost estimates out of kilter. Finally we decided to go ahead anyhow and hope for the best. We reasoned that there must be a few people in the country who were snobs enough to want to be able to boast that in this terrible year they could still spend two hundred and fifty dollars for a book. Not only that, but we also felt that there might well be more than fifty of them. We debated various figures and finally settled on a total run of nine hundred and ninety-nine copies, of which nine hundred and twenty-four would be for sale at fifty dollars, and seventy-five at two hundred and fifty.

Our reasoning proved correct. We sold only about six hundred sets of the regular edition before publication, and we still had quite a few sets left in 1938. But we got orders for one hundred and twenty-six copies of the two-hundred-and-fifty-dollar edition, and we actually had to cut the bookstore orders in order to allocate our seventy-five copies. And this with the depression in full flower!

Thus, in a slightly subdued blaze of glory, ended our adventure in the field of limited editions. It was immensely profitable while it lasted, and I have always regretted the fact that we were never able to issue many of the books we had planned and contracted for. The *Lawn Bank Keats*, for instance, would undoubtedly have taken its place among the truly scholarly works of our times. Helene Perdriat's *Madame Bovary* would have been recognized as the perfect wedding of illustrator and book. And there were many others that had real reason for being. But for the balance of our corporate life, book bargains were all that the public wanted and could afford. We still continued to publish an occasional limited edition, but these were usually specially designed copies of books that we were issuing in a regular edition at a very reasonable price. And a hundred and fifty copies was our absolute maximum, with a good part of these remaining unsold in almost every case.

Actually we went to the opposite extreme. We started to reissue our previously published limited editions in trade editions at very low prices. By the fall of 1933 we were offering reprints of limited editions we had originally sold for as much as twenty-five dollars in a special dollar series. It made the buyers of the original editions very angry, but we didn't care. They were probably not buying even dollar books by then.

This revolution in our publishing plans was not entirely our idea. It came from an efficiency expert we invited into our firm on a contractual basis to help us reorganize ourselves. We chose a man who had absolutely no publishing experience, we agreed to put ourselves very completely in his hands, and we set him up in one of the partitioned offices where he could observe all that was going on. And then we sat back with a smug feeling reminiscent of an associate of Covici in the Chicago days who, as he attached his signature to a note for a bank loan to take care of some pressing commitments, remarked casually and gaily:

"Well, thank God that's paid!"

A few weeks later we were going around in a daze. The publishing business is unlike any business in the world. There is some question in the minds of many publishers if it is actually a business at all. I am not talking of boom times like the twenties or of the even more fantastic wartime boom, when publishers bought up other publishers merely in order to be able to use their paper stocks. Anybody can sell anything in times like those. You don't even have to be able to read to be a publisher. All you need to do is to pay a larger advance than anybody else will offer, spend lots of money on advertising, hire a good publicity man, and hope that your paper will hold out for the reprintings you will require. But in difficult times publishing is a challenge. It is your guess against the public's whims, your sense of anticipation of trends against their actual development, your ability to distinguish between the real and the shoddy against the customers' infallible ability to make this distinction. That's what makes it exciting. But that is also what makes it impossible for a publisher to answer even the simplest of basic questions by an outsider in such a way as to satisfy a questing but uninitiated mind.

And that was the problem we were up against now. Our efficiency expert answered each of our dogmatic statements about publishing practice with a questioning "Why?"— and we couldn't answer him. We knew that things had to be done this way. We knew that we had to back our judgment if we felt that a book had a chance of selling, or turn down another book if we felt that it would not sell. We knew that each new book we published was, in the last analysis, the equivalent of starting a new business, and that when its sale had run its course we would be out of business on that particular title. We knew all these things —but how to convey them to a man who merely asked "Why?" over and over again?

From his point of view he was, of course, completely right. There are few intangibles in banking, or in most other businesses. There are no unpredictable critics who can dismiss a book in one scathing paragraph in the same issue of a book section in which your full-page advertisement calls this same book "a work of sheer genius." There are no earnest book-store clerks who develop an antipathy to a certain book because it says something with which they do not agree. In fact there are no book stores in other businesses—which is a good thing in a way. A grocery store run the way the average book store is run might easily carry only one daily token bottle of milk—because the manager happened not to like milk.

But all these intangibles, and many more, make up the business of publishing. And the experienced publisher allows for all of them, or for as many of them as he can think of. Our poor efficiency expert was continually being baffled by the fact that we actually seemed to be selling books, in spite of the fact that we also seemed to be violating every known rule of common sense. He was with us for six months, and they must have been as trying for him as they were for us. He made a few feasible merchandising suggestions, and a great many more that were not; he straightened out our very involved banking position; and he put through some much needed cuts in salary—starting with Covici's and mine. Outside of that he did nothing—except to start to think that he too was now a publisher. It was when he wanted us to undertake a series of regional books on New Jersey—his home state—and kept bombarding us day after day with facts and figures to prove to us that this was the way to make real money, that we decided the time had come to buy up his contract and part company. It was only after he left us that we realized that the money we had paid him would have gone a long way toward maintaining our salaries at our previous levels.

On his last day at the office he came to each of us in turn and very ceremoniously said good-bye. And we were so glad to see him go, and so anxious to be rid of all memory of him, that we all pitched in, the minute he had gone out the front door, and ripped his office apart, restoring it in less than ten minutes to the state it had been in before he took it over. The last traces of his late occupancy of the space had just been removed, and we were surveying the scene gleefully when we were startled to see him coming in through the front door. He had, it seemed, forgotten his umbrella. I have never seen such a hurt expression on anybody's face. And I have never felt quite so ashamed of myself as I did when I caught the reproachful look in his eye. After he had left for the second and final time, we sneaked back to our offices like guilty school children. Short of taking him back again, I doubt if there was anything we would not have done to make up for our childish actions.

His departure left us slightly worse off than we had been before. For one thing we had become cautious, and in our condition that was the least intelligent state we could have been in. We had to take chances to survive. And our next move, as radical a departure from all our ideas of publishing as could be imagined, was very definitely a drowning man's desperate gesture.

Until then we had never published a single novel in which we did not believe. Rather, we had never published a novel unless we felt that either the book or the author had some value. Now we decided to publish fiction for that new outlet, the circulating library. Machine-made fiction, written to order around a title, and planned to sell with a minimum of advertising, it was to take the place of our lost margin of profit, the limited edition.

We first came to consider this idea in a very odd manner. One day I happened to think of a title, *Speakeasy Girl*, and of what a really interesting story could be written about the young girls-about-town for whom the speakeasy was practically home. I spoke to some of the people in the office about this idea, and they were all enthusiastic. They agreed that it would make a very salable book. In order to see how the idea would look on paper, we sat down then and there and wrote our blurb for it. "There is a new kind of girl in America," it began. "She arrived on the scene with Prohibition and she has now come of age. She is as immoral as she is wise, as pretty as she is young. The speakeasy is her office, just as the saloon was once her father's club. All men are her playfellows, all women her enemies. No one knows how she lives, but the secrets of no man's life are safe from her. Her wits and her face are her stock in trade—and she is the shrewdest trader that ever walked the Main Stem. This is her story, told in the unvarnished language of a girl whose knowledge of her heroine was not born of mere observation. A smashing story of New York's brightest lights and darkest pleasure-haunts."

"Wow!" we said when we read the blurb we had written. "This is really quite a book." We handed the blurb to an artist—if I remember correctly it was Alajalov—and told him to make us the most eye-catching jacket he could produce. He did. And then we took a double-page spread in the *Publishers' Weekly*, complete with a cut of the jacket and our blurb, in order to get the book-store reaction.

We got it all right, and it was good. But we got something else too, something we had not expected. Every motion-picture company in America was after us for a copy of the manuscript from the minute the one advertisement appeared. And much as we would have liked to oblige them, the fact remained that we could not, and for a very simple reason. There was no manuscript. There was, as a matter of fact, nothing except our blurb and a very handsome jacket. We had not even settled on who was to write the book for us.

114

This project was finally undertaken by a very well-known writer, who agreed to deliver the completed manuscript in six weeks, and did so. But I have always had reason to suspect that he could easily have given it to us six weeks sooner. I will never believe otherwise than that it was a book his secretary had written and had asked him to place for her. It was very bad. It also, unfortunately, had nothing to do with our blurb. It was the sordid story of a gangster's moll, and of how she was rubbed out for knowing too much. It was, in other words, merely a blown-up rewrite of a story you could read almost weekly in the more sensational newspapers.

But we had managed to get a very good advance sale—helped along somewhat by one thousand aluminum cocktail shakers, each with the jacket of the book pasted on them, that we had sent to all the buyers and chief clerks in the leading book stores. And maybe, we thought, some picture company would buy the book for the title. So we rushed the manuscript through and hurried proofs to the picture companies, and we very carefully managed to avoid sending advance copies of the book to the book stores. And although nothing happened with any of the studios—except for the fact that one company made a picture called *Speakeasy Girl* a few years later and quite properly pointed out to us that you could not copyright a title and therefore they owed us nothing for using it—the bookstore sale was good, probably because nobody, having bought the book for its title and blurb, could ever dare admit how badly he had been had.

Even before *Speakeasy Girl* appeared, we had made plans to have others like it written for us. We could tell a good thing when we saw it, and this certainly seemed to be at least part of the answer we, and our creditors, were looking for. In the next year and a half we brought out at least a dozen similar books, each aimed for the same market, and each published with our collective ears waiting to hear the rustle of motion-picture money, a sound, by the way, we never did hear. The titles were all vaguely alike—*Bachelor's Wife*, *Boy Crazy*, *Her Body Speaks*, *The Sportsman on the Sofa*, *Alimony Jail*—and so were the books. In fact the best description I can give of any of them is a line from a blurb George Joel wrote about one of the later ones. "Out of a plot so slight that to detail it would contribute nothing . . ." he began. But I think I have made myself sufficiently clear.

The whole thing came to a head one day late in 1932. We had just received copies of our monthly statement, and it was obvious that our sales of popular books were dropping to a point where we were no longer making any money from them. Covici called a meeting, and he wasted no time in coming to the point. "Gentlemen," he said, indicating the statement, "the time has come for a change in policy. If we must lose money in publishing, let us at least lose it on good books." And that was the end of our one and only attempt to play to the popular circulating-library market.

Yet even while we were publishing these incredible books, our list also included such other works as Dr. George M. Priest's translation of *Faust*, Horace Gregory's translation of Catullus, Gene Fowler's *The Great Mouthpiece*, books by Morris Fishbein, Ilya Ehrenburg, and Franklin D. Roosevelt—this last a collection of speeches published by us in June 1932, thereby clearly enabling us to qualify among that select group that was "for Roosevelt before Chicago"—and Ben Hecht's novel, *A Jew in Love*.

There was a fine bond of affection between Covici and Hecht. In their Chicago days they had pooled their talents and their pennies in various hilarious and utterly impractical schemes. And when Covici moved to New York we jointly took over the pleasant pastime of publishing Hecht.

116

And publishing Hecht included not only publishing his novels and his short stories and his produced plays but also things like printing an unproduced play of his called *Christmas Eve*—it was subtitled "A Morality Play"—in a special edition of one hundred and eleven copies, none of which was for sale, as a Christmas present for our friends.

All of this was, of course, before Hecht's Hollywood days. After the success of *The Front Page* he was wooed and won by an offer of more money than he had ever made in his life, and he came to Hollywood often and proved beyond any possibility of doubt that he was as much of a craftsman in that field as in any other to which he chose to turn his hand. But nonetheless Hollywood was for money only as far as he was concerned. Writing was his craft, and writing meant plays and short stories and novels—all written in the magnificent home he had built for himself on the banks of the Hudson in Nyack.

For some time now, between trips to the Coast, he had been working on what he felt would prove to be his magnum opus, a huge, sprawling, panoramic novel for which he was using the working title of *Deliaga*. One of the minor characters in it was to be a composite picture of a publisher and a poet and a theatrical figure, to whom he gave the name of Jo Boshere. But the colorful Jo refused to remain a minor character, and it soon became obvious to Hecht that the whole book was slowly becoming dominated by him. So he pulled him out of the book entirely and wrote a long short story about him, under the title of *A Jew in Love*. This was to be the lead story in a collection of Hecht's short stories that we planned to publish. But when Covici read the manuscript he got terribly excited about the title story and suggested to Hecht that he expand it into a novel. We could, he pointed out, publish the other short stories the following season. Hecht agreed, and we began to get weekly progress reports from Covici, each more enthusiastic than the previous one. It was a great book, he assured us, by far the best thing Hecht had ever written. We would see just how great it was when we read the completed manuscript. It would not be fair to it, he said in answer to our requests that we be permitted to see some part of it, to read the book until it was finished. We would just have to be patient. He even refused to tell us what it was all about.

The result was that when the manuscript finally reached us we were panting with excitement. We all cleared our desks of any work that happened to be facing us, and soon four of us were reading the book, passing pages of manuscript down the line as each finished reading them. And suddenly, at about page one hundred, we all stopped as if on a signal. We looked at one another and we could see that we were in agreement. We did not like the book. And we were certain that the more we read of it the less we would like it. And yet it was our lead book for the spring and a certain big seller. Something had to be done about it, and at once.

We went to Covici's office and told him what we proposed to do. We would not read any more of the book. That much was definite. And we would try to forget how much we had disliked what we had already read. There were still four months before we would have to go out and sell it. We would spend that period of time in a Couélike trance, telling ourselves and each other what a great book it was, how infinitely superior to anything Hecht had ever written, what a certain best seller it was bound to be, how lucky we were to be publishing it. We did a pretty good job of persuading ourselves. Our advance sale was the biggest we ever had on any novel, and we ended up by selling close to fifty thousand copies of the book, a phenomenal sale in those days—and an excellent one at any time.

There was a hilarious aftermath to this mass self-hypnosis act. I had told my wife how we all felt about the book, and what we were doing to combat this feeling. And I refused to let her read an advance copy. But once it was published and well on its way, I brought home a copy, and she took it with her to read on the train to Washington one day when we were going down there for the week end. She read for about an hour, and then she slammed the book shut. "I think this is terrible," she said. "I don't want to read any more of it." I looked up from the book I was reading, and quite automatically I protested. "Don't be silly," I said, "it's a great book. It's infinitely superior to anything Hecht has ever written. I think we're lucky to be publishing it." It was at this point that I noticed the smile of amusement on her face. I grinned at her and turned back to my book.

Our next phase—the deadly serious, if-it-isn't-proletarian-it-can't-be-good phase—was now ready to make its appearance, but we were still quite unaware of this fact. Actually we got into it quite accidentally when we accepted John Strachey's *The Coming Struggle for Power*. We liked the book and wanted to publish it, but we did not expect much of a sale for it. As a matter of fact, our first printing consisted of exactly fifteen hundred copies. We were completely taken by surprise when it became a best seller. But it opened up a whole new vista of publishing for us, and in the next few years we were to publish some of the best books we had ever undertaken, although they were all pretty much on one note. Among them were three more books by Strachey; Robert Forsythe's *Redder than the Rose*; a biography of Karl Marx and a selection of his writings on art and literature; two books by Diego Rivera: *Portrait of America* and *Portrait of Mexico*; and four books of the American scene: *Revolt among the Sharecroppers*, *Revolt on the Campus*, *The Decline of*

American Capitalism, and *America Faces the Barricades*. There were novels called *The Plebeian's Progress* and *The Disinherited* and *A World to Win*. There was even a children's book, *Hans Sees the World*, in which Hans gets his picture of America from Bill, a young American boy whose father is a wealthy munitions manufacturer. And there were also Clifford Odets's first plays, *Waiting for Lefty*, *Awake and Sing!* and *Till the Day I Die*.

It was almost inevitable that we should have undertaken the publishing of Odets's work. We went to see *Waiting for Lefty* in a small theater on lower Fifth Avenue, in a performance given as a benefit for the striking taxicab drivers. And we saw one of the most remarkable performances of a play ever given, an occasion where the audience became a part of the play on the stage. It was tremendously effective and tremendously moving. We decided to offer Odets publication at once.

After the performance we all went downtown to my apartment in the Village, Odets and Covici and Heywood Broun and half a dozen others we had managed to gather up along the way. And we sat and drank and talked in the living-room that Henry Varnum Poor had built for me out of tulipwood inlaid with strips of lead, with a built-in bar in the corner. Or rather Broun talked and we listened, and no one more intently than Odets himself, sitting quietly in a dark corner, never saying a word. After the others had left we made our deal with him, agreeing, among other things, to issue *Waiting for Lefty* in a special inexpensive edition. Odets insisted on this. Copies of this play, he said, had to be made available to the people for whom it was written.

With the publication of Odets we closed our actively leftish phase. Bennett Cerf, whose ear is constantly pressed close to the ground where he can detect the slightest tinkle of a cash register ringing up a sale, had persuaded Strachey, earlier in 1935, that Random House could do a better job for him than could poor shaky Covici, Friede. Now, after reading the reviews of the published Odets plays, he came to us and offered to buy our contract with him. At the moment we were in no position to give Odets the advertising that Cerf promised him, and it seemed a shame to jeopardize his future for selfish reasons. Besides, we needed the money we were being offered for the contract. We sold— contract, stock in hand, bound sheets, and plates. We could not know it then with absolute certainty—although we did all of us suspect it—but we had less than three years of life left in us. What we definitely did not know was that those last years would always be remembered by us as the "John Steinbeck Era."

A
DECENT
FUNERAL

*L*ooking at our auditor's monthly reports—I have kept a full set of them as an object lesson on the dangers of overoptimism—I am astounded at our ability to survive the various crises we came through. We poured money into what came to resemble a bottomless pit, we sold some of our stock to our associates and to our relatives, and still we could never manage to overcome the shock of having had to write off all the money we had invested in our limited-edition department, in the good old days of Coolidge prosperity. Now, in the summer of 1935, our situation became really desperate.

We had pared our office force to the bone, we had all of us taken further salary cuts, we had moved to less expensive offices. And yet we were faced with far more current liabilities than we could possibly cope with. Covici performed miracles of juggling, paying something to this printer and a token payment to that paper house, but it was finally evident to all of us that even his financial genius could not save us. Something much more drastic would have to be done.

It finally took the form of our putting ourselves completely in the hands of our largest creditor, the J. J. Little & Ives Company, printers and binders who had extended us very liberal credit and who now, by getting all our printing and binding business and putting a tight snaffle rein on us, hoped to be able to recoup their losses. They did not ask for any editorial control of any kind. All they wanted was complete access to our financial transactions. We were delighted to oblige. We were even happy to take additional salary cuts. We wanted to see the firm survive. We had all of us become very fond of it.

And one of the reasons we liked it as much as we did was the fact that we had just published our first book by Steinbeck, *Tortilla Flat*. This delightful book, in which we had so very much confidence, had repaid us by becoming an immediate best seller. Of course we had pulled a few tricks to bring about this desirable end. We knew that all of his previous books had been truly fantastic failures. We knew that the manuscript of this one had made the rounds of almost all the publishers before Covici, tipped off by that astute bookseller Ben Abramson, had asked Steinbeck's agent, Mavis McIntosh, to let us see it. We knew that the trade and the critics might easily classify it as a collection of short stories rather than as a novel. But nevertheless we were completely sold on it. The question was, how could we assure it of success?

The answer, we finally decided, lay in giving it a distinguishing format and in making sure that the first-line critics read it. We were absolutely certain that if they did they could not help but feel about it as we did. After much deliberation we hit on a scheme that seemed to us to solve both problems.

To lift it out of the ruck, we decided on having it illustrated—a most unusual procedure in those days of deep depression, when manufacturing costs had to be watched with a hawklike eye. And who better to choose as an illustrator than that excellent artist Ruth Gannett? For in addition to being really good, and well equipped with the sense of humor the assignment required, she was also the wife of Lewis Gannett. And we were certain that not only would he read the book, but that the other critics, out of deference to him, would read any novel his wife had illustrated. And that was all we wanted. We had no thought of influencing people. We merely wanted to win friends for the book.

Which was exactly the way it worked out, with the result that Steinbeck finally got the push that he needed to put him on the best-seller list. And, even with the all too feeble help we were able to give him in the next few years, he has stayed on it ever since.

But outside of Steinbeck our lists in those last years were not so exciting as we would have liked them to be. True, they included Walter Pach's wonderful edition of *The Journals of Delacroix*, and Maury Maverick's autobiography, and fine biographies of the Du Ponts, the Guggenheims, and Sir Henry Deterding. But there also appeared on this list such books as *Beauty Begins at Home, or How to Make and Use Cosmetics*, and a book on graphology called *Handwriting Tells*. And there was a book called *From Harlem to the Rhine*, written by one of the commanding officers of the 15th Infantry, the New York Negro regiment in the first war. His name was Colonel Arthur W. Little, and he was, by a strange coincidence, the president of J. J. Little & Ives.

There was one other book that, while it did not sell very many copies, still more than paid its way. It was written by George Ross, then the assistant dramatic critic on the *World-Telegram*. He also wrote a column on restaurants and night clubs which he called "Tips on Tables." This column made it possible for him to eat and entertain in any place in town, on a completely legitimate basis: if the food or the entertainment was good, he would say so, with a resulting increase in business for the proprietors; if it was bad, he would simply not mention the place.

Ross loved books, but on the rather small salary he received he could not afford to buy them. We at Covici, Friede, on the other hand, loved the theater equally well and could afford it even less. We soon worked out a fine and equitable system. We supplied Ross with all the books he wanted, and in exchange we got good seats for any play we wanted to see. We might have to wait for a few weeks to get tickets for a smash hit, but it never took any longer than that.

That was the way it started. But we loved good food and an occasional night club quite as much as we loved the theater, so we soon decided to carry things one natural step further. If we were to publish a book by Ross on eating and drinking in New York, we reasoned, we, as the book's publishers, should be just as legitimately entitled to free tabs as he was. Besides which, there was a definite need for such a book in those early days of repeal. The speakeasies were coming out into the open, new places were opening every day—and who was to tell the out-of-towner where to go? Ross naturally reacted favorably to the idea and made no objection at all to our setting ourselves up as an advisory committee to accompany him on his rounds of research. We ate well that year. We went to some excellent cabarets. And we sold quite a few copies of the book itself, as a title for which we used the name of his column. The only trouble was that the restaurant business was in a state of flux at the time, and less than a year after the book was published, it was as outdated as a congressman's pre-election promises.

It did make a very nice remainder though. In those days the fabulous Max Salop was the remainder king, and we were his most devoted subjects. We knew that all we had to do was to call him and he would arrive, ready to pay us hard cash for thousands of copies of our books, copies we had printed overoptimistically, or, as happened in a few cases in connection with our reprints of our limited editions, copies we had printed very deliberately, knowing that we could at some time or other avail ourselves of this market. It was rumored that Salop could not read. I cannot vouch for this. I do know that his method of selection was very simple. He would pick up a book and heft it. If it was too light he would shake his head and put it aside. But if its weight pleased him he would nod. "One thousand copies," he'd say, or "Two thousand," or "I'll take them all." We took the hint quickly. All through this period we bulked our books as much as we possibly could. Some of them were practically printed on cardboard and bound in sheets of lead. And if some of Salop's checks read: "One Tousand Dolars," it did not matter in the least: they were as negotiable as any legal tender.

By means of these various devices we managed to keep going. But we almost came a cropper at the very beginning of this period. *Tortilla Flat* had spent such a very long time making the rounds before it found a home with us that Steinbeck had already completed his next novel before we had published the previous one. We were thereby faced with a problem. It was our feeling that with *Tortilla Flat* Steinbeck would finally begin to sell. But it was quite possible that we could be wrong. And the book that was submitted to us a few days before *Tortilla Flat* was to appear, and with which we would have to follow the heart-warming and hilarious story of Danny's house in Monterey, was as different from it as any two books could be. *In Dubious Battle* was hard, grim, and dramatic, and in the last analysis a proletarian novel. And, we were informed by someone in the office who was in a position to know whereof he spoke, it would meet with a very dubious reception from the buyers of such books. It seemed, our informant told us, that it went completely counter to all the currently acceptable Party ideas. And if they turned thumbs down on it, then who, we asked ourselves, would buy it?

We were still debating this problem when we discovered that our hand had been forced in a most unexpected way. Acting on his own, and without so much as discussing it with anyone else in the office, our informant had written Steinbeck a long letter, explaining to him in detail how utterly preposterous *In Dubious Battle* was from the Communist point of view, and informing him that we could not possibly publish it. After which he got around to telling us quite casually about what he had done. It did not seem to disturb him in the least. He was completely convinced that nobody would publish the book.

It took us less than twenty-four hours to discover how wrong he was. Another publisher, we found, was more than willing to publish *In Dubious Battle*, even without having any options on any future books. And that gave us to think, and furiously. We knew how limited our advertising appropriations would have to be. Every penny we spent would have to be spent in direct relation to possible sales. We were in no position to take full-page advertisements merely to impress an author. And if the other firm did do just that, then where would we be when we came to the end of our contract with Steinbeck? If anybody in the office knew him and had a chance to talk to him, that would have been different. But at that time our dealings with him had been mostly through Mavis McIntosh, supplemented by a still only tentatively warm correspondence between Steinbeck in California and Covici in New York.

We argued it out heatedly in an editorial meeting the next day. We decided that we liked *In Dubious Battle* and that, Party line or no Party line, we wanted to publish it. We called Mavis McIntosh and told her of our decision. We wired Steinbeck to ignore the letter that was on its way to him. And then we made very certain of the fact that our adviser would no longer be in a position to try to make us conform to Party ideas. We have often shuddered since then at the realization of how very close we came to losing Steinbeck almost simultaneously with the publishing of our first book by him.

It was shortly after this—Harold Strauss had moved up from the manufacturing department to the post of editor, *Tortilla Flat* had been published and enthusiastically praised by all the critics, our fall list was full of its last major complement of books with the words "revolt" and "crisis" in their titles, Max Salop was finding us his most reliable source of supply, and J. J. Little & Ives was in full control—that I took stock of my position and decided that the time had come for me to make a change. It was obvious that there was no longer any reason for me to remain with the company I had helped found. I was the only childless executive of the company, I was temporarily unmarried, and I was still only thirty-four years old. If I removed myself from the picture I would relieve the firm of my salary—infinitesimally small now, but still a salary —and besides there was just not enough work to be done to keep all of us busy. Furthermore I did not enjoy evaluating manuscripts for their value as possible remainders, or publishing them merely to prove to another publisher that the author really was salable and should be wooed at once with a large advance check. All in all, publishing had ceased to be the exciting game I had known it to be. I decided to quit. I disposed of my stock to my associates— they were to pay for it in small weekly installments— bought a car, sublet my apartment, and drove off across the country to Hollywood.

It had been my hope to divorce myself completely from both my firm and from the publishing business. But I soon found that there is no such thing as a divorce from publishing. And even while I struggled through the mystifying jungle of Hollywood, trying to keep my footing in spite of the strange undergrowth that continually blocked my way, I welcomed all the news I could get from the spouse I had tried to desert. I was filled with happiness when Covici wired me that *Of Mice and Men* had been chosen by the Book-of-the-Month Club, our first book-club selection. I proudly watched it climb up on the best-seller list. I was excited by the beauty that Elmer Adler got into the limited edition of *The Red Pony*, a throwback to the day when you could still make a profit out of honestly produced books. And, in mid-1938, I felt that we were safely past the dangerous shoals when our tenth-anniversary list announced such books as Walter Pach's *Memories*, Irving Fineman's *Doctor Addams*, new novels by Ben Hecht and Ludwig Lewisohn, a collection of short stories by John Steinbeck—and promised for the spring of the following year a new novel by Steinbeck tentatively entitled *L'Affaire Lettuceburg*. I began to feel even more nostalgic about publishing than I had in the last three years.

And then one day late in the summer I got a wire from Covici: Little & Ives had called a creditors' meeting for the following week, and planned to throw us into bankruptcy. He suggested that I come on to New York, if I could, in order to protect my remaining investment in the company—a substantial part of my stock had not yet been paid for, and therefore still remained in my control. Within two hours I was in my car, driving East.

Covici had given me no details in his wire, and there had been no preliminary warnings that this situation might arise. It was only after I got to New York four days later that I found out what had happened. Our spring list had been quite weak, and we had lost money on it. One of the books we had counted on for that list had been delayed until fall, and another one, Jack Kirkland's dramatization of *Tortilla Flat* had been withdrawn from the list after it had already been set up. It received probably the worst press that had ever greeted any play, and ran up the staggering total of five performances before it quit by popular demand. To top it all, Steinbeck, dissatisfied with *L'Affaire Lettuceburg*, had withdrawn the novel and had given us a collection of his short stories in its place. His next novel, he had told Covici, would be a very long novel about the Okies. It would be ready for spring 1939 publication.

Colonel Little had been worried by our sad showing, and had asked Covici to come to his office to discuss the fall list and its possibilities. And Covici had found himself up against the same problem of explaining the intangibles of publishing that had so plagued us in connection with our efficiency expert. He had struggled manfully for a while, giving the Colonel conservative estimates of the sales we might expect on the various titles. And then he had hazarded his guess on the sales of *The Long Valley*, Steinbeck's first published collection of short stories.

It was at this point that the Colonel had exploded. He produced the manuscript we had sent to Little & Ives to be set up, and shook it under Covici's nose. "Look at it!" he said, pointing to the sheaf of bedraggled papers he held in his hand. "Look at those filthy pages! It is obvious that this book has been turned down by every publisher in the country. And you dare to tell me that it will sell more than ten thousand copies!" In vain Covici tried to interrupt him, to explain that when it had been decided to publish this collection, Steinbeck had not bothered to have the manuscript retyped but had merely collected, from all the magazines that had published these stories, the original manuscripts from which they had been set. Of course they were dirty and bedraggled: compositors are not in the habit of washing their hands between pages. But the Colonel would have none of it. He had had enough, he announced. We were through. He called the creditors' meeting then and there.

Obviously there was little that we could do to stop him. We none of us had any more money to put into the firm, and besides the very calling of the meeting had given us a black eye from which it was doubtful if we could ever recover. The vultures were already swooping around, picking the titles they would like to have for their lists as soon as our corporate body was cold. But we could make sure of one thing: that no manuscript that was not already in work would fall into Little & Ives's clutching hands. We did a good job of it too. I personally drove up to Vermont to give Fineman back the manuscript of his novel and to explain the situation to him. And Covici had a closetful of manuscripts in his apartment—safe from Colonel Little's inquiring eye.

The meeting itself was held in one of the ballrooms at the Commodore Hotel. It was the first and only time I had ever been in one of these rooms, the walls of which seemed to retain the flavor of innumerable conventions long since forgotten. In our case it was like sitting in at our own funeral. And it seemed ridiculously unnecessary, for we were actually far from dead. We had been in many much more difficult situations before, and without the prospects that we now had. We had no way of knowing that *The Grapes of Wrath* would be a Book-of-the-Month selection, an internationally recognized classic, and an outstanding motion picture; but we did know that it would be a big seller in the following list, and that only some last-minute corrections had kept Steinbeck from sending on the manuscript before this. And that one big seller, added to the list we had scheduled for the fall, would be enough to get us completely on our feet again, and maybe even out of Little & Ives's hands.

The proof of how right we were in our reasoning was that in the liquidation of the company every creditor got paid off in full and every author got every cent in royalties that was due him. We were the only losers. We got nothing. Every penny we had put into the firm vanished without trace in the course of the two hours that the meeting lasted. And when our creditors and authors and friends came over to shake hands with us and offer their condolences after the meeting, I could not help but look for the flower-covered casket and listen for the muted organ playing behind the velvet curtain.

After it was all over we scattered in every direction, as necessity forced us to do. But by twos and threes we still get together whenever we can and talk over the good old days. There will not be such days again for any of us—not for Covici, who, with Steinbeck tucked securely under his arm, moved to Viking, where he can finally function as the editor he is without waking up in the morning in a cold sweat, wondering if he is going to be able to get the paper he needs without paying for the paper he has already used; not for George Joel, now vice-president of the Dial Press, even though two books he published in 1946 each sold over one million copies including book-club sales; not for Joe Margolies, back with Brentano's again and even more important now than he was when he left them to come with us eighteen years ago; not for any of the others now with Knopf and Dial and other solvent and successful firms who know that they need never publish a *Speakeasy Girl* in order to survive.

And as I continue to struggle through the Hollywood jungle, still after twelve years picking my way carefully to avoid the lush growth that seems to want to envelop me, I too know that there will never be such days again, and nothing that can ever happen to me will give me the satisfaction of seeing my name on a book—any book—even a limited edition illustrated by Alexander King.

AMERICAN
COMEDY

*T*HERE was another phase of my pub-
lishing life which gave it constant spice and excitement.
The books that Boni & Liveright, and later, Covici, Friede,
published could hardly be called Sunday-school tracts.
They were, or at least they were intended to be, adult publications, written for the sophisticated reader who realized
that the word "fairy" did not necessarily refer to the
sprites in *Iolanthe*. And this fact tended to get me into occasional trouble with John S. Sumner in New York and the
Watch and Ward Society in Boston.

Temperamentally I was always opposed to censorship.
I did not grant anyone the right to tell me what I should
do. This was only natural, since I was living in a period
when the major philosophy of life was that anything you
did was permissible as long as it did not hurt anyone else.
And I did not feel that a book could hurt anyone. I agreed
completely with Jimmy Walker's famous statement at the
hearings in Albany on the proposed Clean Books Bill, a bill
that would have imposed a very strict censorship on the
whole publishing industry. Walker had listened in absolute silence while a procession of blue noses pleaded their
case, quoting at length, and undoubtedly completely out

of context, from all manner of books that they felt should never again be permitted to see the light of day. When they had all had their say, he got up and made one of the shortest speeches on record, and yet one that killed the bill for good and all. "To the best of my information and belief," he said, "no girl has ever been ruined by a book."

I was tried twice in my publishing career on charges of publishing obscene books. Or rather I was tried in connection with two books. The various appeals that were taken brought my court appearances to five. The books were Theodore Dreiser's *An American Tragedy* and Radclyffe Hall's *The Well of Loneliness*. I was defended by Clarence Darrow, Morris Ernst, and Arthur Garfield Hays. And my final batting average was .500. In spite of the most distinguished of counsel, I lost the *American Tragedy* case in Boston, although we did have the satisfaction of knowing that because of this decision the Massachusetts law was changed so that it was no longer possible for that state to exclude one whole volume of a two-volume book as evidence. We won the *Well of Loneliness* case in New York hands down.

The funny part of the *American Tragedy* case was that the book actually never was suppressed in Boston. Early in 1926 the Watch and Ward Society had caused the suppression of the April issue of the *American Mercury*. Mencken and Hays had gone to Boston at once, where Mencken had armed himself with a peddler's license that gave him the right to sell anything he chose except fish, fruits, or vegetables. He took out this license in preference to one that would have given him permission to sell bones, grease, and refuse matter. Armed with this license, he proceeded to Boston Common, where, to the delight of the huge crowd that had gathered to see the fun, he sold a copy of the magazine, for the regular price of fifty cents, to the Reverend Jason Franklin Chase, the secretary of the New

England Watch and Ward Society. It is said that Mencken ostentatiously bit the coin that Chase gave him, although this may be an apocryphal story. In any case he was immediately arrested for selling indecent literature, as was a flabbergasted reporter for the *Baltimore Sun*, in Boston to cover the case, whose sole offense was that he had held the bundle of copies of the *Mercury* while Mencken made the sale to Chase. Nonetheless, he too was booked on the charge of possessing indecent literature.

Much to everyone's surprise, Mencken was acquitted. The result of this eminently fair judicial decision was to infuriate the Boston authorities. After Chase's death—he died shortly after the courts had freed Mencken—the police department took over, and soon it began to seem that no book was safe from their scrutiny. Besides which their methods were unique. They did not bother to suppress books. Rather they merely tipped off the booksellers that such and such a book was in their opinion actionable and could therefore be sold only at the risk of immediate arrest. For a while practically every new book was submitted to the district attorney's office for his opinion on whether or not it was actionable. And if in his opinion it was, it was promptly withdrawn from sale.

Obviously such a situation could not be permitted to endure. There came a day when a package containing some twenty recently published novels, including books by John Erskine, Warwick Deeping, Lion Feuchtwanger, John Dos Passos, H. G. Wells, Ernest Hemingway, Arthur Train, and many others of similar standing and good repute, was sent to the self-appointed censors for their opinion by Richard F. Fuller of the Old Corner Bookshop in Boston. And when the package was returned unopened with the information that henceforth all books would be subject to action without warning of any kind, it was obvious that the time had come for action of another sort.

Among the books in the unopened package was *An American Tragedy*. Since no action had been taken on any of the books in the package Dreiser's novel had, technically at least, not been suppressed. But the question of whether or not it was actionable had been left open. We decided to find out what the Boston courts would say about a situation that made every bookseller constantly liable to arrest on charges brought without warning by authorities who had appointed themselves, without any kind of mandate, the custodians of Boston morals.

Hays and I went up to Boston on April 16, 1927. We made an appointment at police headquarters, and I sold a copy of the two-volume edition of *An American Tragedy* to Lieutenant Daniel J. Hines of the Vice and Narcotics Squad. He paid me the list price of five dollars for the two volumes, and all through the subsequent trials and appeals he continued to wail about the fact that he had never been able to get his money back from the police department. They had pointed out to him that he was authorized to buy dope and dirty postcards in order to secure evidence, but nowhere did it state that he had the right to purchase a book. And they refused to refund his five dollars.

The police department applied for a warrant for my arrest, which was granted, but only after some discussion with the judge. He did not agree with their feeling that the passages from the book which they had submitted to him were obscene. Other passages were submitted, however, and in the end a warrant was issued and a date fixed for trial before the municipal court.

We were surprised that things had gone this far, but we were not the least bit worried. We knew that Judge Devlin of the municipal court would read the entire book himself before he reached his decision. This, incidentally, was something that had so far not been done by either the police department or the judge who had issued the warrant. We were confident that the case would be thrown out in quick order.

As it turned out we were completely wrong. In spite of the fact that the judge had read the book, in spite of the fact that it was shown that the book was used at Harvard in its courses on American literature, *An American Tragedy* was held to be "manifestly corrupting to the morals of youth," and I was therefore guilty of selling obscene literature. We appealed at once.

It wasn't until two years later, in the spring of 1929, that the appeal was heard. And much had happened to me in the meantime. I had left Boni & Liveright, started Covici, Friede, and published *The Well of Loneliness*. When I finally went before the Superior Court in Boston on the Dreiser book, I was still awaiting the results of my appeal against my conviction in New York on charges of publishing Radclyffe Hall's novel, which had been found obscene there. As a matter of fact I had a pretty busy week: the trial in Boston lasted for three days, which gave me just enough time to get back to New York the following morning in time to appear in court there on the other book.

There was a great difference between the situations on the two books. In Dreiser's case there was the seemingly impossible picture of action being taken on a book that was written by one of America's outstanding writers and that had been internationally accepted as a classic. In Radclyffe Hall's case we were dealing with a book that had already been suppressed in England, and that dealt openly with the subject of Lesbianism. We had been pretty certain, even before we published it, that action would be taken on it, and we were not wrong in our reasoning.

We were, however, quite prepared for any action that might be taken. Morris Ernst, who represented us in the *Well of Loneliness* case, had suggested that we should make the opening move. Acting on his advice, I called John S.

Sumner as soon as we had copies of the book, and told him that we would be publishing in a few days and wanted to make sure of the fact that he would not go around arresting innocent clerks in the book stores. We were ready and willing to assume full responsibility for publishing the book, and if he wanted to make a test case of it, we would co-operate fully. If he wanted to buy a copy of the book from me, I assured him that I would be very happy to sell him one. In that way there could be no question about who the defendant was to be. We made an appointment for later in the day at our offices. Sumner came, bought a copy of the book from me, paid me the regular price of five dollars, and left without indicating whether or not he planned to take any action.

It was almost a month before he made a move. I was walking back to the office after lunch one day in January 1929 when I saw one of the girls from the office signaling me frantically from a point a full half block away from the entrance to our building. Sumner and his men, she informed me, were at this moment in our offices, confiscating all the copies of the book they could find in our shipping room. And they had a warrant for my arrest. I was to go to Morris Ernst's office at once.

I did. And with my arrest, one of the most effective legal campaigns I have ever witnessed began to function. Hundreds of wires were sent to doctors, authors, clergymen, critics—in fact to anyone and everyone we could think of —asking their opinion both on the book itself and on the attempts that were being made to suppress it. And hundreds of wires came back from them, all opposing censorship of any kind and decrying it in connection with *The Well of Loneliness*. There were some funny ones too. Sinclair Lewis described the book as "almost lugubriously moral." Edna Ferber, after making sure that we would not use her name in connection with a possible advertising quote, since, as she put it, she did not feel that the book was "sufficiently important, as a piece of writing, regarded from the point of view of artistic or technical achievement, to warrant any great fuss being made about it," nonetheless backed us to the hilt in our fight against censorship on the grounds that she feared that eventually "the New York Vice Society will discover the Old Testament." But the best wire of all came from Eugene Boissevain, Edna Millay's husband. "Will not some true Christian," he said, "teach Mr. Sumner to abuse himself instead of us and thus get rid of all this public nuisance?" I have often wondered about how this telegram ever got through. Somebody at Western Union must have been asleep that day.

We were confident that we would win in short order. We had had a fine critical reception when the book was published, and the list of names of those who felt that the book should not be suppressed included practically every writer of importance in the world. But even while everything was moving along so smoothly and effectively, some of our well-meaning friends were trying to help us out of what they thought were our very real difficulties. And they almost succeeded in getting us into very real trouble.

It was their plan to try to fix the case, figuring that we might end up by losing it after all, in which case we would really be in a serious plight. In spite of our insistence on their not attempting anything of the sort, they proceeded to get in touch with a man who was known as a fixer, with the suggestion that he do his best to arrange things for an acquittal. They did not tell us that they had done this. There would be plenty of time for that, they reasoned, when they were informed that all that remained to be done was to pass the necessary amount of money, probably in well-used bills of low denominations. And when the fixer reported to them that he had been unable to do anything for them, they did not tell us about this either. The result was that we knew nothing about what had been attempted when we went into court in February 1929.

I was so confident of being acquitted that day that I had booked passage to Europe on the *Vulcania*, due to sail at midnight that night. I was therefore completely taken by surprise when the judge glared at me when I stood up before him, and then proceeded to read a scathing indictment of *The Well of Loneliness*, of the firm of Covici, Friede, and of me. It made me feel as if I had been caught selling filthy postcards to school children. The strange part of it all was that what he read was very obviously the work of a scholar, and an excellent one at that, which the judge very definitely was not. In fact, parts of the document were just a little too difficult for the judge to handle. There was one word in particular that seemed to baffle him completely. He came to a full stop when he reached it for the first time, and studied it intensely. Then he plunged on bravely. "As far as I am able to goo-ahg," he read, while we tried desperately to restrain our laughter. It was ludicrously obvious that the judge was meeting up with the word "gauge" for the very first time in his life.

In any case I was found guilty, and we naturally appealed the case to the Court of Special Sessions. It was not until many years later that I found out why the judge had been so very bitter. I ran into him at the Stork Club—he had retired from the bench by then, and was successfully practicing law—and we started to talk about the case. "I did you a favor at that time," he said, "and I didn't mean to. As a matter of fact I was sore as hell, and I wanted to do something to hurt you. Some punk came to me and tried to bribe me before the case came up in court. And he had the colossal nerve to offer me five hundred dollars to dismiss the charge." He snorted. "Imagine it!" he said. "Five hundred dollars! That made it doubly insulting. I wanted to throw the book at you."

As a result of the trial I had to sneak aboard the *Vulcania* that night, and I stayed in hiding until the boat sailed. For company I had two ships' news reporters, and we managed to demolish a number of bottles of excellent champagne that a complaisant steward had brought to my cabin. In fact, we did so very well by it that I shall never forget the experience of handing down the almost limp bodies of the two reporters when the time came for them to attempt the climb down the rope ladder to the pilot's tender, bobbing in the rough February seas.

I got back to New York on Saturday, April 14. I had a very full week ahead of me. On Monday the *American Tragedy* case was due to open in Boston. And on Friday the *Well of Loneliness* decision was to be handed down in New York. I couldn't help wondering if I would be able to play both engagements.

Dreiser, Darrow, Hays, and I took the train for Boston the night I landed. I was to have a jury trial in the Superior Court, and we did not see how we could lose. Boston had been held up to ridicule all over the world ever since the first decision on the book.

But as soon as the jury had been chosen, and the first witness for the prosecution, Lieutenant Daniel J. Hines, had taken the stand, we saw that we had probably been completely wrong. I had sold the two-volume edition of *An American Tragedy* to Lieutenant Hines. At that time it was the only form in which the book was being published. And now we discovered that volume two was never to be presented as evidence to the jurors, nor, for that matter, was the whole of volume one. Only those passages that the district attorney considered actionable, taken completely out of context by him and presented without any thought of continuity, were to be presented to the jury. And they were supposed to judge the book on that basis.

The district attorney read a few paragraphs from page

47 and then a few more from page 60, and then without any explanation of any kind he jumped to page 137 and from there to page 307. So far he had read, at the most, a page or so each time, and in most cases not even a whole page. Now, however, he had reached the section that dealt with Roberta's pregnancy and Clyde's pathetic attempts to do something about helping her get an abortion. Starting with page 379 of the book he read some ten pages of disconnected excerpts of the next forty pages. And then he turned the witness over to Hays. He had completed his case.

Hays had been jumping up and down all morning, objecting, arguing, questioning—and getting exactly no place. When he tried to get around the district attorney by the ingenious device of making the purpose of the book clear to the jury, and of filling in the missing links in what they had heard, he was defeated by the fact that the judge excused the jury while he made his plea. And he was further defeated by the fact that the judge refused to permit volume two to be introduced in evidence, refused to permit the whole of volume one to be introduced in evidence, refused Hays permission to read the first twenty-five pages of the book, in fact refused to do anything but make the jury consider the charges on the basis of the excerpts from volume one which had been read to them by the district attorney.

Finally Hays tried a new tack. He put me on the stand in an attempt to get me to give an outline of the book. "Objection," cried the district attorney. "Sustained," said the judge. "Exception," said Hays. He put Dreiser on the stand and tried the same tactics—and with the same results, or rather, lack of them. Finally he did manage to get the court's permission to read the whole of chapter 7, from which the district attorney had read his first short excerpt. But when he tried to have Dreiser say that in order to understand this chapter it was necessary to have read the opening chapter, there was the same old chorus from district attorney and judge, and the same tired "Exception" from Hays.

The next chapter from which the district attorney had culled his morsels was chapter 9. Again Hays got permission to read the entire chapter so that the jury might, as he put it, have a better understanding of the excerpts from it they had heard. And then he made the perfectly logical suggestion that he really should be permitted to read the intervening chapter 8 so that there would also be established some sense of continuity, this in spite of the fact that the district attorney had read no excerpts from this chapter. The three familiar voices sounded off in the courtroom in the, by now, familiar order.

And so it went—for long hour after long hour. I had actually never been more than just a figure in the court procedure—there had to be a defendant, for you obviously could not send a book to jail—and I had left the courtroom a number of times to go to the toilet, to get a glass of water, to smoke a quick cigarette. But for some unknown reason the district attorney suddenly took it into his head late that afternoon to interrupt Hays's reading of one of the chapters from the book by rising and informing the judge in his most dramatic voice that the defendant was leaving the courtroom. I came to a sudden red-faced stop, freezing into position as completely as any wax statue. And there I stood while Hays with an absolutely straight face requested the judge to permit me to go to the men's room. The judge just as solemnly agreed, provided I return at once. I resumed my temporarily interrupted motion toward the courtroom door.

The next morning Hays tried new tactics. I doubt if he had slept very well the previous night. He was much too good a lawyer to accept such repetitious defeats gracefully. In any case he now called on Darrow in the hope that his arguments might carry more weight with the judge. But it was a false hope, for the judge excused the jury before he would permit Darrow to speak. He made a beautiful and eloquent speech too, one that should have gained Hays his point. But it didn't. The judge listened to Darrow respectfully, and denied his plea as completely as he had denied Hays's. The jury came back, the reading of the complete chapters from which the district attorney had read excerpts was renewed—Darrow was actually permitted to read a whole chapter to the jury—but the intervening chapters and the story of the book as a whole might just as well never have existed as far as the jury was concerned. The judge refused to let anything be done to correct this situation.

Finally we came to the end of the chapters that we were permitted to read, and Hays rested. And Darrow spoke again—to a juryless courtroom—trying to plead the point that a nine-hundred-page, five-dollar, two-volume novel, from which the district attorney had excerpted less than fifteen pages in all, differed in every respect from a copy of *Only a Boy*. It was an adult book, intended for adults, likely to be read only by adults.

"But supposing," the Judge asked, "supposing it did fall into the hands of someone seventeen, eighteen, or nineteen years of age?"

"Well now," said Darrow, hitching up his galluses, "let me give you my view on that. There are precocious boys and girls, and 'precocious' means just what the word implies, older than the almanac says. Of course there are people who have lived, according to the almanac, fifty years, that are not ten years old; and there are some seventeen or eighteen that know more than most people would know if they lived forever. And supposing I were to concede that one or two young people might take a bad meaning from the book. You can't make all the literature in this world for the benefit of three-year-old children, or ten-year-old children, or fifteen-year-old children. It is utterly absurd. We cannot print all our literature for the weak-minded and the very immature."

It did no good. But then by that time we had come to realize that nothing would do any good. And certainly we did ourselves no good by what we did that night. The papers were full of that story in the morning, and the reporters covering our case told me confidentially that it would prove to be the last straw. After that we didn't have a chance.

Actually all we did was to attend a meeting given at Ford Hall in honor of Margaret Sanger, then still fighting desperately to win her battle for legalized birth control. She had been informed by the authorities that she would not be permitted to speak at the meeting, and there were policemen there to make sure that she did not. And when at the end of a laudatory speech she was introduced and rose to take a bow—the only method permitted her to acknowledge the applause—she very deliberately and ostentatiously placed a large piece of adhesive tape over her mouth. Then she stood while a speech was read by someone else at the speaker's table. The police were nonplused. She was obviously not disobeying the law, for there she stood, not saying a word, her mouth securely taped. And by the time they realized they had been tricked and that the speech that had been read while she stood there silently was actually the speech she wanted to deliver, it was too late: the speech was ending and Margaret Sanger was sitting down again and removing the tape from her mouth.

After that Darrow had made a speech, and so had Dreiser. And there had been some skits, including a very funny one about the current position of the Boston bookseller. The papers reported that the "Bookshop skit brought down the house," and they went in for some pretty fancy headlines in covering the speeches. "Boston Hit by Liberal's Wit" was one of them. "Bad Book Author Ridicules Censorship" was another. All in all it was obvious that we might expect even more trouble from the district attorney than we had already had from him.

We soon discovered how right we were in feeling as we did. Hays addressed the jury—with the usual interruptions from the district attorney. He had not yet given up all hope of being able to tell them what the book they were judging was about.

Then the district attorney got up to deliver his speech to the jury. It began—it actually began—with the landing of the Pilgrims on Plymouth Rock, and pretty soon it started to refer to stage acts we had come over to put on in "their little village." "The only thing, that is missing in their act," he continued, "is Texas Guinan herself." He switched to the subject of obscenity then, and he gave it the works. "I know not," he said, "where they get their notions of obscenity; I know not, sirs, from whence they derive their sociology or philosophy by which they determine what is obscene and what is not; I know not whether they are going to bring you to the jungles of Africa. But I got my notions, and I know you got yours, sirs, at your mother's knee when she prayed that you would be pure in thought, pure in word, pure in actions."

He was off now. He took up each one of the excerpts he had read, and asked the jury how they would like to have their fifteen-year-old daughters read that. He read about the girl in the brothel who had started to undress when she and Clyde were alone in her room. "Well," he said, giving the word all he had, "perhaps where the gentleman published this book it is not considered obscene, indecent, and impure for a woman to start disrobing before a man, but it happens to be out in Roxbury where I come from." There was a lot more along the same lines, and then there was a final crack. "Do not worry, sirs," he said. "I will not keep you much longer. I promised to finish before four o'clock. I am on salary, I am not by the day, so I will be through on time."

We were not much surprised when the jury brought in a verdict of guilty. We immediately appealed the case to the supreme court of the Commonwealth. We lost the case there too in time, and I finally had to pay a fine of three hundred dollars for my heinous crime. Actually I was given a choice of a fine or of ninety days in jail, and for a while I toyed with the idea of becoming a martyr. Besides, I felt that a nice long stay in jail would give me a chance to get caught up on my reading—I was particularly anxious to read Proust slowly and without interruption. But I decided against the jail term and paid the fine. And I had the satisfaction of knowing that the law was changed after this trial so that it was no longer possible for a book to be tried on excerpts arbitrarily chosen by a self-appointed censor. The new law made it very clear that the whole book must be introduced in evidence, and that it must be judged as a whole.

After the excitement of the Boston trial, the final act in the *Well of Loneliness* case in New York the next morning came as somewhat of an anticlimax. I stood before three judges in the Court of Special Sessions and listened while the presiding judge delivered their unanimous opinion: Radclyffe Hall's book, they had decided, was not an obscene publication. The case was dismissed.

ELEVEN

AWAY
FROM
IT
ALL

*I*F I HADN'T just returned from Europe before my harrowing week in court in 1929, I probably would have gone there for a vacation after that experience. I welcomed every excuse I could think of to get on a ship, and always preferably a French Line ship, and my passport at all times carried currently valid visas for France, England, and Germany. For years I went abroad on business at least twice a year, and two or three times I even managed to find reasons for an extra trip.

But at the bottom of the depression in 1931, a business trip to Europe was out of the question. For that matter a business trip to Chicago was something you thought twice about—and then probably decided against. That was the summer flagons in New York were apt to be filled, if they were filled at all, with the sharp and pungent "red ink" that was obtainable at Italian restaurants and no place else; apples were being sold on all street corners by shabby men who wondered if they would ever know security again; and I, in common with everybody else, was sick of it all.

I took a year's leave of absence from Covici, Friede, bought a car, and sailed for Europe. There, with the dollar at a premium in all countries, I would find peace and quiet in Paris or on the Riviera, or maybe in that newly discovered heaven for the expatriate with a small but reliable income, Majorca.

I took with me my wife, two cases of books, including a complete set of the *Encyclopædia Britannica*, and a brand new portable typewriter. It was quite possible, I said to myself, that somewhere along the line I might settle down and write a novel.

Naturally I did not attempt it in Paris. There was too much else to do. We took a studio-apartment in a narrow street on the Left Bank, a beautiful place with the obligatory north light streaming in through the huge studio windows, a garden, which it was much too cold for us to use during the months of November and December for which we had rented the apartment, and upstairs a bedroom and a bathroom with the most temperamental water heater I have ever had the misfortune to meet. The rental was ridiculously small, and our weekly check from Covici, Friede—I had put myself on half salary while I was in Europe—was more than adequate for our needs. And the company in Paris was of the best—the back-to-America movement had not yet started, and the Dôme was still a place where to hear anybody speaking French was surprising enough to warrant a frankly curious stare and a whispered "Who is that, do you suppose?" to your companion.

We had a wonderful time. There was a constant round of parties, and visits to the country, and evenings in the cafés, and dinners in little restaurants to which we were introduced by possessively proud compatriots. There was the apartment that one of our friends was so proud of with its four fully equipped bathrooms in a neat row—"These Americans," the landlord seemed to have said to himself, "they like many bathrooms. *Bon!* I shall give them bathrooms, and to spare. But if I put them each next to other, then I shall save money. So that is the way it shall be done." And the Thanksgiving dinner at my wife's cousins', where the turkey was perfectly roasted and traditionally stuffed by an awe-stricken French cook, who nonetheless refused to believe that marshmallow-covered sweet potatoes were meant to be served with the roast, and who brought them in, beautifully caramelized and burning hot, as the logical dessert to follow such a meal. And the wonderful Russian dinner at my cousins' apartment, where we ate continuously for what seemed to be three whole days. And the first big surrealist exhibit, when fights broke out in the streets, between the followers of the two groups that had decided to open shows on the same night, and had had the foolhardy idea to schedule the *vernissage* for New Year's Eve. We were rapidly beginning to think of ourselves as native Parisians.

But that was not getting a novel written, nor was it living the quiet rural life. We had, however, heard disquieting rumors about the Riviera. It was going to have a cold and wet and miserable winter. We must not, under any circumstances, think of going there. The place to go was definitely Majorca. You could live for practically nothing, and besides it was warm and sunny and it still had not been spoiled by Americans. We packed our few bags—most of our clothes and all of our books had been sitting in a warehouse in Marseille for the last two months; waiting for us—and as soon as we could pull ourselves together on the morning of the second of January, we loaded our car and started off.

But we had decided to make a slight detour. We wanted

to go to Italy, to Locarno, to visit Doctor van de Velde, the author of *Ideal Marriage*. From there we would turn south and drive to Barcelona and take the overnight boat to Majorca. As it worked out we ended up in Vienna, which is something like driving from New York to Washington via Chicago. And the trip over the Alps in the middle of January was an experience in terror that has never been equaled in my experience. The roads were so icy that on at least two occasions children skimmed right past us on skates on the road, causing us to come to a dead stop and to debate the advisability of abandoning the car and walking to the nearest inn. When we finally got into the higher snow-covered mountain passes, we found ourselves on laboriously cleared one-way paths, with the snow piled many feet high on the mountain side of the road. Meeting a car coming in the opposite direction called for the most delicate of backing and filling to avoid going over the completely unprotected outer side of the road, with the drops, which we contemplated with increasing nervousness, averaging many thousands of feet in all cases. Six inches was the closest we ever came to going over the edge, but that was too close by many feet. We finally decided to give up and to ship our car through the tunnel well below the top of the pass. At that we had to wait at the edge of the town where we were to put it on a flat car until a snow plow could clear the way to the station for us. We breathed a sigh of relief when we finally saw the car safely battened down under its protective tarpaulin.

The other side of the mountain was warm and snowless, and so was most of the rest of our trip to Vienna. It was cold again when we finally got there, and the roads were snow-covered for many miles. But we could see fields and houses on both sides of us, and that was all we cared about. It was a long time before we ventured to drive on a mountain road again, and when we did we made quite sure that there would not be snow anywhere along the way.

We arrived in Vienna with two suitcases, prepared to spend two weeks. We ended up by staying for three months, and it was the day after our clothes and books arrived from Marseille, where we had finally sent for them, that we left for Majorca, shipping our unopened trunks and packing cases right back where they had come from. They were a wonderful three months.

There was in Vienna at that time one of the most incredible collections of American newspaper talent that has ever been assembled in one place. All the news of consequence was originating in the eastern part of Europe, and Vienna was the logical headquarters for men whose beat included Bucharest and Berlin. Besides which, few of these men had as yet made their mark. They were promising and willing and able, but their by-lines were still not internationally known. They were, however, well on their way.

John Gunther was there, genial and jolly, his home the meeting place for all the visiting celebrities, of whom there seemed to be a constant stream. So was William L. Shirer, not yet the bitter anti-Nazi, but even then one of the very few newspaper men who took Hitler and his devious maneuverings with the proper degree of seriousness. They both made their headquarters at the Café Louvre, the gathering place of all the local writers, where the tipsters sometimes outnumbered the paying guests, and where, if you were particularly unlucky, you might draw the waiter who would tell you that he had been Trotsky's favorite servitor. It had been a one-sided affection, you gathered. In any case, when Trotsky had gone back to Russia he had left owing the waiter a considerable amount of money. From the over-large tips left by compassionate patrons, myself included, I gathered that he had long ago recouped his losses many times over.

Whit Burnett and Martha Foley had just issued their first mimeographed copy of *Story*, and were struggling with the printers to get their second issue ready. Their home was the clearing house for the literary news of the continent, and the Mecca of all aspiring young writers. And they gave the best parties in town, complete with inexhaustible barrels of magnificent beer.

Then there was Robert Best. I met him at the Café Louvre, and it was he who told me how to get the maximum rate of exchange for my dollars, a complicated procedure that at times did not seem worth the many devious steps involved. Having ingratiated himself to me in this manner, he decided that the time was ripe for a touch, and he approached me with a proposition that involved securing from the Austrian archives a mass of secret Metternich documents that, he assured me, were of inestimable value. He was probably right. At least I never did get to estimate their worth. There was a great deal of money passed for the supposed purpose of having secret photostatic copies made, and further monies for the purpose of greasing palms that would permit these photostats to be removed from the archives. But I never saw a single line of all the papers I was supposed to get. After a while I began to realize that I had just purchased the Viennese equivalent of the Brooklyn Bridge. I was not too surprised to hear many years later that Best had lent himself enthusiastically to the Nazi cause and had hired himself out to broadcast for them. He always had about him an aura of availability.

Actually my basic reason for coming to Vienna had been to be psychoanalyzed by Wilhelm Stekel. We took an apartment a few doors away from his office, and I began my daily sessions with him, lying on the obligatory leather couch in a darkened room while the jolly bearded doctor took notes and asked an occasional question. At first all went well. In a matter of a few days Stekel cleared up three seemingly unrelated facts; my fear of cats, my fear of the dark, and a recurring nightmare in which I dreamed that I was awake and lying completely immobile waiting for an unidentifiable but nonetheless terrifying something to happen to me. Traced quickly back to childhood, the three things proved to be completely interrelated. As a child of ten in St. Petersburg I had had a kitten. I had also been given a set of lacquer paints. I had painted the kitten with gold paint one Sunday afternoon while my parents were out, and some of the paint had got into its eyes. In agony with the pain, it had jumped out of the window to the courtyard six floors below. I had burst into tears, and my governess had made me go to bed to await the punishment my father would mete out to me. And there I lay in the dark, dozing off occasionally, exhausted by my continuous crying, waiting for I knew not what to happen to me when Father came home. And, seemingly, I still lay in bed awaiting his return and his punishment.

This simple re-creation of a scene that had evidently stayed in my subconscious all those years cured me of both my basic fears, and I never had the nightmare again. But otherwise we did not fare so well. As a matter of fact, our work together came to an abrupt end after less than one week. We had reached the stage in our work together when, in order to get a clearer picture of what exactly made me tick, Stekel was subjecting me to the ordeal of a session of free association, a series of questions on completely unrelated subjects which I was to answer unhesitatingly with the first answer that occurred to me. All went well for a while. I answered the first queries with satisfactory promptness, and Stekel scribbled away busily at his desk. And then came a very simple question. What book, the doctor asked, had had the greatest influence on my life? I did not hesitate for a second. *"The Pickwick Papers,"* I said, almost before he finished. There was a momentary pause, and then I sat up and Stekel swung his chair around to face me. We looked at each other and smiled. He closed his notebook carefully. "You are a very nice fellow," he said. "I shall enjoy seeing you while you are in Vienna. Maybe you will go ice skating with me. But," he continued, "there is no point in our wasting each other's time professionally any longer. Do you agree?" I did. We shook hands cordially and parted the best of friends. And that was the end of my psychoanalysis.

But it was out of the question to write a novel in Vienna that winter. There was entirely too much to do. There was the corner café, with its newspapers and billiard table and excellent food and superlative coffee, available in fifteen or more different combinations of coffee and milk and cream and mounds of whipped cream. I was informed that due to the sedentary life led by the Viennese all café coffee had a small quantity of an extract of fig added to it, making it unnecessary for the regular patrons to worry about their continuous lack of exercise. I discovered that this applied to sedentary Americans too. And so we would spend hours in our café, or in any of the hundreds of others in town. Occasionally we would manage to get up enough energy to go out of town for a leisurely dinner at some inn that had been recommended to us. But we resolutely avoided invitations to go skiing. It sounded entirely too strenuous.

There was wonderful music in Vienna that winter, and magnificent opera, with the Vienna Philharmonic in the orchestra pit, and exciting sets, which helped you to overlook the fact that the singers were not exactly of the best. In fact they were pretty bad. The cost of the orchestra and the sets had made such a dent in the budget that they could not afford to hire good singers. It did not seem to matter: I got seats in the ex-royal box for the greatest performance of the *Ring* I have ever heard. For the only time in my life I heard the music as it was supposed to be played. And the be-capped and be-aproned Habsburg relic who stood outside the ladies' room waiting for customers, and the huge refreshment hall crowded with burgers eating frankfurters and drinking beer where in the past champagne had flowed freely, contrasted with each other as sharply as did the plain straight-backed chairs in the ornate box where Franz Josef and Rudolf of Mayerling fame had sat at ease in the armchairs and sofas that had been its standard equipment.

And of course there were parties. They ranged from costume balls that did their best to imitate the Beaux Arts Ball in Paris, to quiet evenings at the Gunthers', where the conversation and the guests were both exciting, and you were as likely as not to meet the world's greatest expert on rockets or our ambassador to Hungary, Nicholas Roosevelt, who seemed to spend as much time in Vienna as he did in Budapest. Whenever he was in town you would find William Bullitt there, ready, he announced, to leave the beach he had retired to after the Versailles Peace Conference, and to jump back into politics once more. The Democrats would be back in power again after the fall elections, and that was when he would get his chance. He played it cautiously though. I saw him in Paris later in the year, when the Chicago Democratic Convention that was to nominate Roosevelt for the Presidency had almost run its course. I was surprised to see him in Paris at that time, and I told him so. Had I been wrong, I asked, in thinking that he would surely have wanted to be at the convention? Or was it perhaps that he had changed his mind? Not at all, he said. He had not changed his mind. He was sailing for America that night. By waiting until after the convention had made its choice, he explained, he had avoided committing himself to someone who might not get the nomination. I was forced to agree with his reasoning. It was a magnificent example of opportunistic thinking.

We might easily have stayed on in Vienna for the entire time of my leave of absence if Whit Burnett had not suddenly been notified by the newspaper for which he worked that, as a move in an economy drive they had been forced to make, they were regretfully dispensing with his services. That meant that the Burnett family, complete with their infant child and the new issue of *Story* that was even then on the press, was stranded in Austria with no hope of anything but occasional feature articles to keep them going. Gunther and I got together to see what we could do, and it was decided that I should cable Covici to find out if he wanted to take over the publishing of *Story* in America. His very emphatic answer that he was already having all he could do to keep our collective heads above water took care of that suggestion fully and finally.

It was then that we all began to think about Majorca again. With the exchange rate at twelve to fifteen pesetas to the dollar, it sounded like a true paradise. We began to make inquiries, and the more we investigated the better it sounded. But the prospect of moving four adults and an infant, our cases full of books, which were expected from Marseille momentarily, and all the equipment that was needed for *Story*, together with all of the Burnetts' paraphernalia, all the way across Europe in my Chevrolet convertible roadster, was one we found appalling. It was finally decided that I should go ahead and scout the situation. If I found things as agreeable as I had been told they would be, I was to get a house and servants and notify my wife and the Burnetts, and they would come down by train to Barcelona.

There were a series of farewell parties—including the one at the Burnetts' when we thought we had run out of beer and went dashing out in the middle of the night to get another barrel, only to discover when we came back triumphantly with it that someone had repaired the pump on the still three-quarters-full barrel we had thought was quite empty. The neighbors, I was told later, all got buckets of beer the following morning, with Burnett's compliments.

But by the time this happened I was well on my way south.

TWELVE

DOLLAR PARADISE

A short time after I got to Majorca I was driving in the outskirts of Palma when I noticed a young boy standing by the side of the road. He was about ten years old, and he was waving a Republican flag and shouting alternately: *"¡Viva la republica!"* and *"¡Viva Alfonso!"* His reaction was typically Majorcan. This island, a comfortable overnight trip from the Continental mainland, seemed to be as completely detached from the reality of the rest of the world as if it were on another planet.

Also, I soon found out, the reports we had had of how cheaply you could live there were, if anything, understatements. For the best room in the best hotel in town, complete with a luxurious bathroom and a marble balcony that hung over the first truly blue Mediterranean water I had ever seen in some thirty years of occasional sights of it, I paid three dollars a day—and that included five huge and delicious meals. Everything else was in proportion. It was obvious that this was the place for us, and I wired Vienna at once. The Burnetts and my wife could come down as soon as they wanted to, I said. I would have everything arranged before they arrived.

As a matter of fact, I almost rented a private peninsula for us. It included a beach house and a private beach and a magnificent private chapel. The main house was a marble structure, perched on the edge of a steep cliff and resembling nothing so much as a Habsburg palace—which is exactly what it was. It had belonged to one of the archdukes who had moved to Majorca late in his life and had died there even later. The whole estate—it must have included at least two hundred acres—could be rented unfurnished for twenty dollars a month. It seemed like a wonderful idea—the idea of a mile-long peninsula for our exclusive use appealed to me strongly—but there was one handicap.

The living-room was a truly beautiful thing, with enormous French doors opening onto a marble terrace, and with a fireplace big enough to handle not one ox, but two or maybe even three. But directly in the center of the room there was a marble structure that not only dominated the room, but also managed most effectively to divide it into completely useless halves. I spoke to the caretaker about this. Would it not be possible, I asked, to have this thing removed? I would be glad, I hastened to add, to pay both for removing it and for restoring it after we left. But as he could see— He interrupted me haughtily. Impossible, he assured me. His Highness's will had provided that his body must never be moved. I must have looked as bewildered as I felt, for the caretaker unbent enough to clarify his remark. Didn't I know, he asked, that that marble edifice in the living-room was the archduke's tomb? I made my excuses politely and elaborately, and gave up any idea of renting a peninsula—complete with private chapel and private archduke.

My search for a house took me all over the island. I spent the night in the ex-monastery where George Sand and Chopin had lived—I was assured that I slept in the room they had occupied—but I was unable to rent the building itself. Another American had already taken it, for twenty-five dollars a month. I tried to call on Robert Graves to get some advice on houses from him, but I was warned in the café of the little seaside town in which he lived that this would be dangerous, since as often as not he would set his dogs at strangers. I crossed the island, visited Genevieve Taggard, and had a wonderful time sailing for hours on an enormous land-locked bay and meeting the colony of hopeful young writers who had settled at this faraway point. But there were no printing presses here, and *Story* had to be published. So I went back to Palma and started to look for a house. I had come to the conclusion that I would have to settle for a house that actually resembled a house: all the more exotic structures seemed to be already occupied by compatriots who had preceded me.

I finally found exactly what I wanted. It was perched on the side of a mountain almost a thousand feet above sea level. To the right my nearest neighbor was eighteen miles away. To the left she was appreciably nearer—actually the house that Rudolph Valentino's widow, Natasha Rambova, occupied was less than two hundred yards from our front gate. But these were the only two places in this particular section, and from the upper of our three terraces, which was reached by one hundred and sixteen steps, the view was breath-taking. The Mediterranean sparkled at our feet for as far as the eye could see, and ten miles away to the left the town of Palma shone brightly, the huge cathedral on the water front towering over the smaller buildings.

The house itself consisted of seven large rooms and a kitchen, which was fully equipped with the usual Majorcan stove—a beautiful tile affair with three small cooking surfaces, each of which had to be well and continuously stoked with charcoal. There was no bathroom. There was no icebox. There was no electricity. There was no hot water—one cold-water tap in the kitchen supplied all the running water there was. The toilet facilities were in a small room just off the kitchen and consisted of a marble one-holer. There was a beautiful garage under the lowest terrace, but there was no way of getting to it by car from the road some hundred and fifty yards below it. This mansion was set in a ten-acre grove of fig and almond and orange trees—and it rented for ten dollars a month. I took it at once.

The next step was to furnish it. I did this—including beds, linens, dishes, an ice chest, lamps, and all the furniture we needed—for a total of just under sixty dollars. I was told that I had paid entirely too much. I was told the same thing about the couple I hired. I agreed to give them fifteen dollars a month, and the local American population objected strenuously. The established rate, they assured me, was ten dollars. If I was not careful, they said, I would spoil the natives.

There were a few other things I had to take care of before the others arrived. I bought a lead-lined tub, the kind the English use in the colonies, an object three feet in diameter and a little over a foot high. I put it in one of the bedrooms, and got an enameled two-gallon container with a shower head and a pull chain to control the flow of water, which I mounted on the wall directly over the tub. My houseman and I experimented with it, and we finally discovered that a full gallon of hot water, heated in a kettle on one of the charcoal burners, together with a scant gallon of cold water, supplied water of exactly the right temperature for a shower. I had to buy a stepladder for him to climb on when he filled the shower, and it took the two of us to carry the filled tub out of the house to empty it. But at least we had a shower, which was more than most of our friends could say. It was temperamental though. You had to be very careful not to use too much water in moistening yourself or you would face the danger of finding yourself covered with soap, and with no water left with which to rinse yourself off.

My wife and the Burnetts arrived and were enchanted with the house. But there was one difficulty, and I set about correcting it at once. My cook spoke only French, and when we tried to translate our favorite recipes for her we found that our French was not sufficiently fluent for this purpose. And there was not a single French cookbook to be found in any of the local book stores. I placed my order for the finest one that could be obtained, told the book store to have it rushed to us as quickly as possible, and sat back to wait for its arrival.

Two weeks later it came. I did not even bother to open the rather large package the bookseller handed me, but drove home as fast as I could and gathered the whole household around me. Now, I said, we shall really eat. With Berthe's natural aptitude for cooking and with this fine book to guide her, we shall feast three times a day. I tore off the wrapping and opened the thick book at random. Then my face fell. The first words I saw were "Take an Ox." It was a hotel cookbook, designed for fifty or more servings. And here we were with our three charcoal burners.

We set up the offices of *Story* in the garage, and we started to look for a printer to handle the job. We found one easily enough, one of the oldest craftsmen on the island, but he had just enough type to set up four pages of the magazine at a time. These, he informed us, would have to be corrected, the four pages printed, and the type would then be distributed and four more pages set up. There was no choice in the matter, so this was agreed to. But we were in for a rude shock when the first batch of proofs arrived.

We had all of us completely forgotten that there is no "w" in Spanish, and so the printer had improvised and set up a series of "vv's" in their place. It was an interesting effect, but barely legible, and Burnett regretfully informed the printer that it would not do. He would have to order some "w's" from the mainland. In the meantime the magazine would have to tread water.

The "w's" were ordered and duly arrived—right at the beginning of a protracted longshoremen's strike. For two weeks we looked longingly at the packing cases piled on the dock. In one of them, we knew, were our "w's."

The strike was finally settled, the "w's" were delivered to the printer, and the four pages were laboriously set up again. There was no mistaking the fact that this time the printer's font included them. In fact they were just about the only letter we could see. These brand new letters stood out screamingly on all the pages, in startling contrast to the weak impression made by the other tired-out type. We had to break up the pages again and carefully age the "w's" with delicate hammer poundings. And only then were we finally able to go ahead with printing the magazine.

But that was just part of our life. The island was teeming with Americans—a number of them were refugees from the then current Seabury Investigation—and there was a constant stream of visitors.

Edna Millay and her husband appeared on the island one morning, and were greeted by almost the entire colony at our favorite café. They had come, they announced, to walk across the island. If they liked it they would find a house and stay. Six days later they were back in the café again. They had walked across the island. They had walked back. They had not liked what they had seen. They were taking the night boat back to Barcelona. They would try Spain itself now. Maybe, they said, they would like it better. They left that night without ever explaining to us what it was that they did not like about our island.

But most of us were not so particular. We lived wonderfully well on practically nothing at all, and the climate was good, and the wine was cheap and plentiful. What more could you ask for? Even the local police seemed ready to go out of it's way to cater to the foreign colony. Certainly, in the case of one writer who was inclined to come home to his hotel very late every night, and also to be roaring drunk when he did so, they showed a tactfulness that was extraordinary. There was a flock of peacocks at his hotel, and he had carefully practiced imitating the horrible noise they made. As soon as he got within half a mile of the place he would let out a series of peacock shrieks, and the birds would wake up and answer him call for call. The night was hideous with sound, and the police could do nothing about it. After all, there was a limit to the number of nights on which they could accommodate this man with a cell in the local jail, and besides, they had found that if they put him in jail he would spend the whole night practicing his calls. The other prisoners rightfully objected. They were, they informed the authorities, entitled to a good night's sleep. Nor was it possible for them to cut the writer's vocal cords: it might have provoked an international incident. So they did the next best thing. They cut the peacocks' vocal cords. And after a few abortive attempts to get an answer from the now silent birds, the writer gave up. He left the island soon after this, and I have often wondered if he went in search of more peacocks, all of them in full possession of their noisy faculties.

Actually there was not the amount of drinking that would normally be found in a colony of artists and would-be artists on an island where their money was most welcome. It may have been the climate, it may have been the realization that a world would soon end for them, it may have been just a reaction from years of escape *by* liquor. Whatever the reason, there was very little drunkenness in Majorca—little, that is, in comparison with the drinking that went on in America. We used to meet on the terrace of the leading café in Palma every morning, and we would sit there drinking brandies for an hour or so, making very sure that the waiter filled both our glass and the saucer that went under it. Only if that had been done, the liquor sloshing around in the saucer being poured into our glass after we had drained it, did we feel that we had been given full measure. We would meet there again in the late afternoon for more brandies. And once Burnett and I discovered a bottle of real absinthe and sat for hours sipping it slowly, completely unaware of the passage of time, or of the fact that we were getting very drunk and in a peculiar way. It was only when we tried to take a short cut home by driving the car up a long flight of marble steps that we realized that we might have had a drop or so too much.

There was another reason for patronizing this particular café. It was the only place in Majorca where steaks could be obtained. And we could be very certain of the fact that they were actually beefsteaks, and fresh ones at that. The management was very considerate of its patrons. It had a standing arrangement with the local bull ring whereby all the animals killed there would be delivered to them at once. All the regulars would make a point of dashing for the café right after the fights, and would sit there drinking, waiting for the steaks that would start to make their appearance on every table of the jammed café no later than two hours after the last bull had been killed. There was an added fillip to my last steak dinner there. We had seen the three greatest bullfighters in the world—Lalanda, Barrera, and Ortega—put on a truly magnificent show, and I had just barely managed to duck the bull's ear that Ortega had tossed in our general direction after having

167

been awarded both ears and the tail of his final bull for his superb performance. I had pulled away as the bloody object came sailing at me, but Burnett had reached across me and caught it. And now as we ate our steaks the ear was proudly displayed in the center of our table, the blood that had dripped from it staining the napkin on which it was enthroned. We couldn't help wondering if ear and steaks had come from the same animal, which added to our excitement if not to the enjoyment of our still steaming not-so-tenderloins.

It was while we were having our morning drinks at the café one day that Burnett and I had the idea of getting our combined families on the steamer which was leaving for Minorca in a few hours, and spending the week end with Elliot Paul. We got in the car, rushed home, and hurriedly packed the few things we would need. We had just enough time to wire Paul to meet us at the dock, and to catch the boat as it was getting ready to cast off. All afternoon as we sailed on the glasslike sea we talked about the wonderful food that Paul would have waiting for us, and the beautiful evening he had undoubtedly planned. It came as a great shock to us therefore to find, when we arrived in Minorca late in the afternoon, that there was nobody on the dock to meet us, and no way for us to get to Paul's Spanish town of Santa Eulalia that night. We would have to wait until morning, that is, unless Paul was even then on his way.

He didn't arrive that night, or the next morning either. That, we found out later, was not too strange: our telegram was not delivered until late in the following week, and by that time we had been back home for four days. We had no way of knowing it then, however, and we were not particularly happy about what we thought was his unforgivable lack of consideration. This was particularly true when we found that the hotel situation in town was extremely bad, and that all we could get in the way of accommodations for the seven of us were two stifling bedrooms, each with a large double bed. It was much too hot to think of sleeping in them, so we took the bedding up on the roof of the hotel and made up the necessary number of beds on the comparatively cooler concrete. It seemed to us like a happy solution of an unhappy problem.

But there was one of us who did not join us on the roof. We had visiting us in Majorca a young cousin of mine, whom I have always thought of as one of the most uprooted people I have ever known. She was born in Russia, and spent her early childhood there, surrounded by nurses and governesses and all the luxuries money could buy. And then after the revolution she and her family had managed to escape to Paris with their lives and very little else. Irene had grown up there, still the *jeune fille* she would have become in Russia, still pampered to the best of her parents' ability to pamper her. When I had come dashing home earlier in the day to tell our household that we were leaving in half an hour and to pack a toothbrush, she had taken me literally. We discovered when we got on the ship that a toothbrush was all she had brought with her. And when we dismantled the room and struggled up to the roof with the bedding we had managed to collect, she did not come with us. As a well-brought-up *jeune fille*, it did not seem proper to her to join the mixed group that would be sleeping in the cool air. She chose to retire in a bedroom, as she had been brought up to do. We didn't argue with her. We had come up against every possible variant of her conditioning in the short time she had been with us. We stretched out on the roof and hoped that she would not stifle in the steaming room.

It started to rain in the middle of the night, a sudden torrential downpour that soaked us through and through before we could get ourselves and our bedding down the narrow steps from the roof. And yet wet as we were, we could not help coming to a full stop when we turned the corner of the corridor and arrived at our rooms. There, neatly placed next to each other, just outside the door of Irene's room in this overcrowded and understaffed fifth-rate hotel, were her espadrilles, placed there by her before she went to bed, as she had been taught always to do with her shoes when she stayed at a hotel. The fact that there was nothing that could be done about cleaning espadrilles, even if there had been someone there to attempt it, had never occurred to her. Shoes were shoes, and they were always left outside the door to be cleaned by somebody while you slept.

She went home to Paris shortly after we got back to Majorca, and I never saw her again. But I did have news of her some years later. A short time after the war ended I was officially notified that she, her mother, and her grandmother had all been put to death by the Nazis in the gas chambers of Belsen.

We took a car to Santa Eulalia the following morning, and we spent two wonderful days there. It was easy to see why Paul felt as he did about the place, and we hated to leave it then fully as much as he did under different circumstances a few years later. I have often thought of how prophetic it was that there should have been a German destroyer coming in to the dock for a landing just as we boarded our ship for the trip back to Majorca.

I left Majorca in August for the trip back to New York. I had been told by so many people, including Edna Millay, about the joys of traveling by freighter that I booked passage on one with my fourteen-year-old brother-in-law, whom I had to get back to America in time for the opening of the school year. I made one great mistake though: I booked on a Spanish freighter, and as we swung along the Spanish coast from Barcelona, stopping at every port on the way, I began to realize how very great my mistake had been. The ship was filthy. The stateroom we occupied looked and smelled as if it had not been cleaned for the last three or four crossings. The bathroom, with its cold running salt water, would have been scorned by any self-respecting pig. And the food was inedible. We were served two five-course meals a day, one at ten in the morning and one at five in the afternoon. They were identical, and each featured a bowl of hot olive oil in which pieces of fish floated around unhappily. We came to rely on the cheese and crackers we had somehow thought of buying in Barcelona. These and an occasional bowl of soup were all we ate during the twenty-eight days our crossing lasted.

By the time we had made our fifth stop, at Malaga, we were both heartily sick of the whole idea. But there was nothing we could do about it now. However, we did find out that our ship would not sail from Seville, its final stop before it headed across the Atlantic, until six days later. We packed a few things, took a bus to Algeciras, and from there caught a boat for Africa and Tangier. We tried to store up on all the good food we could eat in the three days we spent there, and we headed back regretfully for Algeciras and the bus that would take us to Seville and our sea-going flop house.

The trip across Spain in the broken-down bus we drew, and on one of the hottest days I have ever experienced, was a long and almost unbearable nightmare. We managed to doze off after a while and were very much annoyed when we were awakened in the middle of the day in the main square of the dustiest and most stifling town I could remember seeing and told that this was where we changed buses. We grumbled and got out and, still half asleep, went in search of the only thing which we felt could get the taste of dust out of our parched throats—ice cold Coca-Colas. We found them too, much to our surprise, and we must have had at least five apiece. And then we climbed in our bus, a duplicate of the one we had been on all morning only, if anything, slightly more broken down. But we managed to get seats on the shady side, and that was all that mattered. It was only when we were about to leave, and the doors of the car finally swung shut, that it occurred to us to wonder where we had just been. As we drove out of town and into the blazing countryside again, we found out that we had stopped for half an hour in Jerez de la Frontera, the town that gave its name to sherry, and where not only this wine came from, but also the Spanish brandies, which we had for months been drinking with such great pleasure. The chances of either of us ever finding ourselves again in this out-of-the-way town were exactly nil. And we had used up our half-hour in it in downing ten ice cold Coca-Colas.

There was to be one more frustration before we finally sailed. We got to Seville much later than we had expected to and we were half afraid, half hopeful that we would find our ship had sailed without us. But it was still there when we got to the dock. As a matter of fact, it did not sail for five more days. There had been an abortive revolution while we had been in Tangier, and we sweltered at the dock for a hundred and twenty more hours, waiting for the railroad situation to right itself again so that we could load the freight that was to have been picked up in Seville. In addition to which the ship had just been sold to new owners, and we watched them paint out the old name and paint in the new one. It did not occur to us that this change in name would bewilder our friends and our family back in New York when they tried to find out where to meet us when we docked there. It did though. For a while they could not figure out what had happened to us and to our ship. As a matter of fact they were quite as much puzzled by this last bit of Spanish whimsy as they were by the first sight of my long and flowing beard, the growing of which, early in my stay in Majorca, I had managed to keep completely secret from them. It was not a great success in America though. I shaved it off five days after I landed.

The novel? I finally got around to writing it fifteen years later, and it was pretty bad. It is locked in the bottom of my trunk, which is the best possible place for it.

THIRTEEN

A
MILE
A
MINUTE

*J*UST before the war—the first World War, that is, the one that was to make the world safe for democracy, and was to weld all mankind into one big peace-loving family with the ancestral home permanently located in Geneva—Vernon and Irene Castle introduced tea dancing to an eager audience of more or less mature people who welcomed this new opportunity of escaping the responsibilities of home and office. The pulpit denounced them roundly, both the Castles and their followers. But the latter ignored the clamor and flocked by the thousands to the dozens of places that opened almost overnight in a vain attempt to keep up with the demand for a good dance floor and a good orchestra and a constant supply of young dancing partners for those unfortunate ladies whose husbands were realists enough to recognize their own limitations.

They could not know it then, these desperately carefree parents, but when they placed the seal of respectability on tea dancing they were making a move that would in time

lead to their losing every hold on their children, and would
result in a mounting crescendo of shrill bewildered protest
that echoed from coast to coast for the next fifteen years.
In this one thing their children followed them, and it was
probably the only time they did not automatically reject
every idea their elders considered desirable. And in following them they gained their freedom, and having gained it
they never gave it up again.

It wasn't, however, until the fall of 1918 that the
younger generation, not yet lost or even dimly aware of
the fact that it would soon put on a mantle of sophistication to hide the shabbiness of its shallow ideas, moved in
on the sacred purlieus of its mothers and fathers. It took
a war to bring this about, a very polite war in which, it
was true, a number of people died, poison gas was used,
and some cities were tentatively bombed. But behind the
rather static lines of the long trench-warfare stalemate,
things went on pretty much as usual. And across the
natural barrier of three thousand miles of ocean, safe behind this impregnable wall, life took on a carnival feeling,
business boomed, and conventions went by the board. And
looming large among the casualties that never appeared in
the newspaper lists, or on the monuments that sprang up
all over the country on peaceful courthouse squares, was
the chaperone.

Not that she gave up the ghost easily. Far from it. She
hung on for a number of years, mortally wounded, dying
by inches, fighting every minute of the time. But it was a
losing battle. It was as good as lost the first time girls of
good families were permitted to dance with boys without
parental or other supervision. True that was in the after-
noons and therefore comparatively respectable when
viewed in the light of standards that were still only one
step beyond those of the Victorian era. Doubtfully at first,
and then with increasing resignation, permission was

granted these nice girls to go dancing alone with boys, but always with the admonition to "be home before it gets dark, dear." It was as if there were some magic quality in daylight which would protect a girl's chastity. But after a while even that doubtful protection was denied this priceless jewel. When parents began to say: "Don't be home too late, dear," the battle was really lost, and the weary chaperone, exhausted by her useless struggle, closed her eyes and breathed her last.

All this happened in my time. I was almost eighteen years old when I took my first girl tea dancing. We met under the clock in the Biltmore, at the head of the flight of stairs that led up to the lobby from the Forty-third Street entrance. It probably never occurred to us to meet any place else. Well before five each day the lobby began to fill up with very young men, each of them convinced that he and he alone looked calm and collected and many years older than his actual age. They would consult their watches, checking them carefully against the clock in the alcove with its leather benches, and, unable to find a seat in this constantly crowded spot, they would begin to pace up and down the lobby, keeping their eyes vigilantly on the stairs, as if it were actually possible for them to miss seeing their girls as they ran breathlessly up the long steps.

Week end after week end I would be among them, watching the sacred stairs even as I pretended to talk to a classmate or a friend, darting an occasional glance at the long hallway that led to the Vanderbilt Avenue entrance on the off chance that my girl might be coming in that way. Or we would cluster around the cigar counter at the side of the lobby, and sometimes we would buy gold-tipped Egyptian cigarettes, lighting them with an affected nonchalance that our inept handling of the heady smoke denied to even the most casual of observers. Or maybe we would light a pipe, holding it aggressively in our mouth,

trying to make it seem as if this were what we really enjoyed in the way of a smoke, and trying at the same time
to control the wave of nausea that would roll over us if we
did not knock the half-smoked pipeful of tobacco into the
sand-filled containers soon enough. The truth of the matter
was that we smoked very little at any time, and then only
mild cigarettes like Egyptian Deities or Melachrinos or
Pall Malls. But we would have denied this under torture.
According to us we all smoked at least three packs a day.
And some of us were even beginning to affect those cheap
cigarettes, Lucky Strikes, which had become such favorites
with the men in the Army. This was even more likely to
be the case if we wore wrist watches. These still smacked
of effeminacy to most people, and we had to be doubly
virile to assert our right to wear them. And somehow we
felt that the plain tips on the cigarette in the green-and-
red package established that fact much more clearly than
did the cork tips of the cigarettes we found much more
enjoyable.

A few minutes after five the girls would start arriving,
the plainer and more timorous ones first and then prettier
and still prettier ones. The belles of the day would be the
last to appear, fluttery with apologies that gave them a
chance to draw all eyes to them as they made their self-
assured way up the stairs, well aware of the stir they were
creating. Then there would be a rush for the room from
which the strains of the polite music, which had started
long before, could be heard clearly in the lobby, and a quick
order given to the waiter—tea and cinnamon toast was the
usual thing, or maybe hot chocolate "with plenty of
whipped cream"—and then we would be out on the floor,
moving happily and sedately among the others in the inevitably overcrowded space.

If your girl was pretty, and if she was building a reputa-
tion as a prom-trotter, you could be very sure of one thing.

The stag line would descend on you en masse, and if you got more than halfway around the floor with her, you could consider yourself lucky. That was all right with you: far better to have that happen than to make dreary turn after dreary turn around the floor, trying to catch the always averted eyes of all of your friends, giving up after a while and going back to your table to the cold toast and the tepid chocolate. That meant that the stamp of approval had been denied your girl, and she knew as she munched her toast and tried to amuse you that you would never take her out again.

Within a few years we had all moved over to the Plaza Grill, meeting at the foot of the steep stairs that led from Fifty-ninth Street directly to the table at the entrance of the Grill Room where you bought your tickets. It was always exciting to go down those stairs. As you came in the door you could hear the music playing dimly and you could almost smell the perfume on the eager girls waiting in the marble lobby, or peering into the Grill Room itself while their escorts checked their coats, or coming out in excited twos for some important discussion for which they would have to retire to the sanctuary of the ladies' room. They were all very young and they were all very pretty, and this was their big moment of freedom. There was nobody to tell them what to do or whom to dance with or whom to cut. This was their room, and they were, for the moment at least, grown-up and free.

The boys were mostly from the Eastern colleges, and they tried very hard to seem blasé and worldly. This, they seemed to be saying, is just a childish diversion. You should see me in New Haven or Trenton. I'm a real heller there. Actually they were enjoying themselves hugely. They knew these girls well, most of them since childhood, and they knew what was expected of them and what the rules were. In Trenton or in New Haven they would often find themselves at a disadvantage with the townies. But that could never happen to them here.

By the time the Plaza Grill and later the Club de Vingt had become the places to go, many of us had come to an important decision. We rarely took a girl tea dancing, preferring to stag it whenever we could, joining any group that appealed to us, dancing with any attractive girl we saw on the floor. As a matter of fact the girls at these dances were most of them regulars, the current crop of prom-trotters who did the circuit of the colleges every winter and who came here during week ends and vacations just to keep their hands in. Usually they would come with some young hopeful, who would be beaming with pride at having been selected as the escort of the afternoon. But soon he'd be a very disillusioned young man: his table would become the center of an eager group, and if he tried to dance with his partner to escape, he'd manage only a few steps before he was cut in on. Some of them, however, never seemed to learn, for which we wiser ones had good reason to be grateful.

Joe Smith would be playing as we came in, his round fat face beaming over his violin, and he would bow to us as we danced past him on the jam-packed floor in a way that made us feel grown-up and accepted. This was terribly important to us, trying as we were to be sophisticated and clever. But above all, we were at that time trying to remain consistent to our "lines," those rigidly personalized codes of conduct that governed our thoughts, our actions, and above all, our words. We all had lines then, boys and girls alike, projections of what we thought we were or what we thought we wanted to be, a form of carefully rehearsed dream world. We would brief each other on new lines we had run into from new girls, and no successful prom-trotter would ever think of going to a dance without a full course of instruction on the lines of the men she would meet and dance with. It was in a way a modern version of the stylized gallantry of the Victorian era, an attempt to create for ourselves a pattern of speech and action that by constant use and repetition would enable us to say and do things in the way that would least involve us. In any case we used to spend a great deal of time and thought on our lines and in studying those we saw and heard all about us.

By mid-1920 something else had happened that was to influence us profoundly. *This Side of Paradise* had been published, and all the young men saw themselves as Amory Blaine and all the young girls wished desperately to be everything that Fitzgerald's girls were. That book set the pattern for the mood of the day, and it also laid the solid foundation for the basic philosophy of the whole decade. When Amory decided that we were members of a new generation, grown up to find all Gods dead, all wars fought, all faith in man shaken, we gasped our acquiescence. We had been fumbling around for this thought, and here it was stated for us, clearly, incontrovertibly, succinctly. We were never the same again. And when a few years later this new race of Fitzgerald's came to be known as the "lost generation," we accepted the label gratefully. With a philosophy of life based on these simple statements, we were free to do as we wished, to live for today, to burn our candles eagerly at both ends, to be deliberately and determinedly hedonistic.

It took time for this basic idea to take full control of us and of our actions. It took time and Prohibition and the Harding scandals, and our own amazing prosperity, and the cynicism of the men who had fought in the war, and the slow realization that we had been dupes at the very moment of our highest patriotic exaltation. All of that came later. But then, in the opening year of Prohibition and of the decade, the first faint stirrings of revolt were beginning to come to a head. We hadn't the vaguest idea of where we were going, but we did know very definitely that for us there was no road back, no return to the ideas and manners of our parents and grandparents.

And it wasn't only new ideas that we were exposed to. The world itself was changing before our delighted eyes. Take the automobile for one instance. Consider its effect on us. Suddenly, almost overnight as a matter of fact, we found ourselves mobile, able to get off by ourselves at any time, or to park under the willows at the fifteenth hole whenever we happened to meet a girl who had similar ideas. Henry Ford must often have shuddered at the realization that he as much as any one person made the whole jazz age possible. Certainly he could have had no inkling of what his effect on the morals of the world was going to be when he and my father met in 1905.

In that year, with the Russo-Japanese war just ended, my father was faced with a serious problem. He had suffered heavy losses in the war when some of the ships of the steamship line he was operating in the Orient had been sunk and others so effectively blockaded that their cargoes rotted and ended up by being a total loss. Now, back in America again, he looked around for a new business in which to invest what was left of his money. But of one thing he was very certain: he would be cautious and conservative this time. After all, his children were growing up—my brother was fifteen years old at the time and I had just turned four—and he owed it to them, he reasoned, not to have them grow up penniless. And so when Henry Ford offered him a quarter interest in the Ford Motor Company for ten thousand dollars, he shook his head regretfully, and turned him down, letting a man named Couzens make the investment in his place. For himself he took the far safer gamble of acquiring the exclusive representation of this new car for all of Russia. He reasoned, and this part of his decision was definitely not open to debate, that only a Ford could negotiate the Russian roads, which at that time were almost nonexistent.

The result was that I was practically weaned on cars. I was driving a Ford in St. Petersburg when I was eleven years old, and I had a license to do so too. I drove with my brother in the St. Petersburg-Kronstadt race, when that fifteen-mile strip of sea froze over in the winter and Fords invariably finished one, two, three. I drove in road races in mud that often seeped over the floor boards, and through deep overflowing river beds. I drove in the Crimea on mountain roads so narrow and twisting that we had to back and fill at least four times to negotiate every corner, with a sheer drop of hundreds of feet at the completely open side of the road.

Back in America in 1916 I had a Model T, and I used to travel with the full complement of tools which had to be carried in those days, and with tire patches and vulcanizing outfits and the absolute certainty that I would have to use most of my equipment before the day's driving was done. Later I used to tool back and forth between New York and New Haven at a steady thirty miles an hour, convinced that this headlong pace was the only way to make the trip. I even felt that way the night the lights of the car gave out right after I had left Bridgeport shortly after two in the morning. I knew that no garage between there and New Haven would possibly be open at that hour. It was a very dark and moonless night, and the flashlight I was carrying threw the kind of almost invisible light that was all the flashlights of the period were capable of. But I knew that there would be practically no traffic at that time of night on the stretch of some thirty-odd miles of road, and I did not turn back to Bridgeport. Instead I drove on carefully, listening intently, trying to stay on the road. When I heard the sound of gravel under my left wheels I would straighten out the car and continue until I heard the sound of gravel under my right wheels, at which point I would bear slightly to the left and continue my zigzag process. I made it, I may add, without incident and without seeing more than five cars in the two hours or so it took me to make the trip.

It never occurred to me that a Model T was not the height of everything that was desirable in an automobile until I went to Princeton. And there I went out one day with a friend of mine in his new car, a Hudson Super-Six, and we drove to the still unopened Princeton-New Brunswick highway and found a stretch of road that was completed. We let the car our. And pretty soon there we were rolling along at sixty miles per hour—an incredible mile each and every minute! It was an unforgettable thrill and it spoiled Model T's for me for all time. And when I drove my first Packard Twin-Six—think of it, twelve cylinders in one car!—I really got the bug bad. I ran through a flock of cars in the years that followed.

I drove a Stutz and a Marmon and a Buick and a Mercer —coming through Elizabeth, New Jersey, one night, I blew six fuses in my Mercer in less than half an hour—and I yearned for a Jordan and a Templar. I drove a Rolls-Royce and I desperately wanted to own a Roamer, that sleek American imitation of the queen of cars. And for five years I thought that nothing could possibly be more exciting than to take a good car out onto the best open stretch of road I could find and let her out, feeling the powerful motor carrying me forward at dizzying speed.

It was during these years too that I first became exposed to flying. I have never once had my hands on the controls of a plane, and yet somehow I feel almost as if I had been a pioneer aviator. In Russia in the very early days of flying we tried never to miss any of the air meets, and I can still see before me the astonishing sight of one of the first Wright planes taking off from its elaborate track in St.

Petersburg sometime before 1909. Later I watched Pégoud loop the loop over and over again at the air field in Moscow in 1914, and begged uselessly to be permitted to go up with him. And I will always remember the thrill I got at the news of Blériot's first successful flight across the English Channel.

Actually I did not make my first flight until late in 1920. And then it was in a seaplane in Atlantic City, and we circled sedately over the boardwalk and the beach. After that I flew whenever I could. I chartered a seaplane in Maine in 1922 when I suddenly decided that I did not feel up to the balance of the trip to my destination over the increasingly bad roads. And the fact that we flew over land most of the way, or over lakes entirely too small for us if the occasion for a forced landing had arisen, bothered me not at all. Nor did the fact that we barely made a landing on the lake we were headed for, and that when we took off for the return trip we missed the tops of the trees by fractions of inches. I flew between Boston and New York and across the Isthmus at Panama. I flew from Pittsburgh to New York in a plane that seemed to graze the tops of the mountains below us, and I flew from Paris to London, and from London to Berlin—as a matter of fact I flew from any place to any place in any kind of a plane and from any kind of field. I thought it was the only way to travel.

All this, of course, was before 1930 at a time when the Ford Tri-Motor was the most advanced transport plane in the world. Mostly the planes I flew in boasted of only one engine and of very few passengers. Schedules were fairly elastic too. The time of arrival, or of departure for that matter, was far less important than the fact that you actually, somehow, did manage to arrive. Much later I was to fly across the country often, sleeping peacefully in wide, comfortable beds on the lightest and most beautiful sheets I have ever known. But I never enjoyed these flights one tenth as much as I did my earlier ones in noisy, smelly, teeth-shaking planes, when drops of hundreds of feet and sudden sickening bumps were part of the whole experience of flying. Somehow anything else seemed entirely too effete.

My flying career came to an abrupt end when I was assigned to the Air Corps in 1942. During the whole of the time I spent in this branch of the service I never once was in a plane. In fact I only saw one plane land in all that time. That was at Sioux Falls, South Dakota, on an incredibly cold February day when we were standing retreat in a thirty-mile wind. A B-17 came in for a landing on the field before our eyes, and the lieutenant who had us in charge, taking pity on us in our miserable state, gave us "at ease." And standing there shivering, we watched openmouthed as a plane, a real heavier-than-air machine, glided gracefully down to the ice-covered ground. We had almost forgotten what an airplane looked like.

YE OLDE RADIO SHOPPE

To THE sound of his own personal portable radio blasting away at his side, the sixteen-year-old boy next door spends all his spare time working on his sleek and shiny hot rod so that he can fill it with high-school girls every night. He would find it very hard to realize that a bare ten years or so before he was born, cars, planes, and joy-riding high-school girls were so rare as to be practically nonexistent. But he might find it equally difficult to imagine a world in which there was no such thing as radio as he knows it, with its pushbuttons, AC-DC-battery sets, built-in aerials, one-control tuning—and round-the-clock relays of disk jockeys.

And yet in 1923 I earned the undying respect of a grocer in Sharon, Connecticut, by fixing his radio with a piece of chewing gum. I very definitely thought of myself as a radio expert at the time. But then so did thousands of others who religiously bought the Friday-afternoon papers for the ten- and twelve-page radio supplements they carried. It was in one of them, by the way, that I saw the advertisement of a new radio store in the Bronx which managed to reach the apex of silly bad taste in its choice of a name. Proudly, and seemingly without any idea of the anachronisms involved, it called itself "Ye Olde Radio Shoppe."

But then everything about radio in those days was pretty silly. Heavy switches and huge and expensive lightning arresters were a standard and obligatory part of everyone's equipment. Indoor aerials were strung along hall ceilings, tastefully mounted on glass or porcelain insulators that could have served equally well on any high-tension lines. Batteries—heavy-duty batteries with their full complement of acid and water and hydrometers to test their condition— stood on pieces of linoleum directly under the instrument-cluttered tables, the clawlike clips that established connection between radio and battery corroding visibly as you watched them. And if you were lucky enough to own a charger, in that way avoiding the weekly carting of the heavy and dripping battery to the nearest battery-charging shop, then you knew that your whole apartment would be filled with an intermittent hum, a cosy and almost supersonic sound that you soon came to accept as a part of contemporary life.

Actually it started quite simply. I bought my first radio, a crystal set with a long coil of wire for an antenna and a set of headphones, in the fall of 1921. I took it up to the top floor of a brownstone house, opened up all the connecting doors, set up clothes trees as far apart as I could get them, wound the wire from tree to tree, hooked in the set to one end of the aerial, took another piece of wire and attached it to a radiator, hooked in the headset, sat with them over my ears for a full fifteen minutes while I fiddled with the cat whisker that was supposed to make contact with the bit of crystal under the glass cap—and then suddenly there it was. I wasn't quite sure of what it was, but it was obviously something: a voice or maybe music, I couldn't be sure which. I handed the earphones to a friend, but I must have jarred the crystal in doing so because when he put the earphones on, there was no longer anything coming through them. He sat there for a while fiddling with the cat whisker. Pretty soon his face lighted up, he motioned for silence, and he smiled up at me. But when he tried to hand me the headset, he knocked the set out of adjustment, and I had to go through the whole routine all over again. And yet it was a thrill I'll never forget, this first faint sound of something coming over the air, caught in the earphones of a crystal set.

Within a few months I had graduated from that stage, and my bedroom looked like the radio shack in a tramp steamer. I had managed to assemble a fantastic collection of units, and had hooked them up on the principle that the more meters and controls and tubes you could string together, the better the reception would be. And I boasted of a real Magnavox horn speaker, a very special thing that required a storage battery all its own. On this impressive outfit I could pick up every local station, and late at night when the Eastern stations had gone off the air, I could get Davenport, Iowa, and Chicago, and once, for a fleeting minute, a California station. And I could and did listen in to the first experiments in ship-to-shore conversations, even though I could only hear one side of the test. But that didn't matter very much. It wasn't what you heard that counted then; it was merely the fact that you could hear at all. I sometimes wonder, listening to the radio these days, if times have changed so much.

It was in the summer of 1922 that I had my great idea. There were, I reasoned, dozens of summer hotels in Maine and similar remote spots which would welcome the idea of entertaining their guests with radio music, especially something good enough to dance to. Instead of the weekly Saturday-night dances, they could have them every night if they wanted to. And the first cost of the machine would be the last one. It seemed ridiculous to me that no one had thought of it before. I decided to set out on a crusade to make Maine radio-conscious. But first I had to find a set simple enough to make it possible for me to guarantee results no matter who operated it. It had to be powerful too, powerful enough to receive music on a loud-speaker, and it had to be in one unit, not counting the two storage batteries it would need and the battery charger, and of course the Magnavox speaker. And it had to operate from a loop aerial, since I would probably run into serious opposition to a long aerial in a part of the country where summer thunderstorms were an accepted climatic condition.

Miraculously I found what I needed. A young radio man on Eighth Street had just begun to build a set that was housed in one large cabinet somewhat resembling a coffin in size and appearance. It was a masterpiece of simplicity too, since it had only twelve controls and three meters on the long Bakelite board. Furthermore it was planned for a loop aerial, a neat and compact one that at its widest needed only four feet to revolve in. I outlined my idea to him, and he approved of it. I agreed to buy one set and take it up to Maine. We were to split the profit on any orders I sent him. It began to look as if I was in business.

But there was another problem. I had to get the set to Maine, and I had to be mobile enough to take it around from hotel to hotel, picking up orders as I went along. And that called for an automobile. It had to be a very special sort of automobile too, since the radio and the batteries and the loud-speaker and all the other paraphernalia I had to take with me were much too large for a rumble seat and far too fragile to be entrusted to the rear seat of the average car. Once more, and miraculously again, I finally found just what I needed. It was a Sheridan, probably the last one of that make ever manufactured. A closed car, it had a most unusual seating arrangement, with the driver's seat backed by a deep storage compartment, and the rear seat, which was about as long as a love seat—or, in this case, exactly as long as my radio—only a foot or so behind the driver. With the storage batteries on the floor in front of this seat, with the set itself securely tied into the seat, with the loop aerial mounted on top of the set, thereby effectively blocking any possible rear vision, with the Magnavox loudspeaker mounted on top of the storage compartment, the edge of the horn a scant inch back of my head, and with extra storage batteries, extra tubes, extra wire, a battery charger, and dozens of other necessary items, each allotted its own special place, my car, when I finally was ready to leave, resembled nothing so much as a Rube Goldberg drawing.

It was, however, to the best of my knowledge, the first radio-equipped car. True there was little place in the car for anything but radio and driver, but on the Staten Island ferry I drew a far larger crowd with my demonstration of mobile radio than the customary blind musician. Because the loop aerial was much too big to swing around in the car, I could only count on good reception when the ferry boat was heading in the proper direction, but since for most of the run it obligingly set my aerial for me in relation to the local stations, I did not have to face this problem too much. It was only when we turned to warp into the slip that the sound faded and died.

It was fortunate for me that I had decided to spend a few days on the Jersey coast before heading north. I found that the rough roads did not agree with the delicate mechanism I was carrying, and I came back to my friend on Eighth Street for necessary repairs. We repacked everything, leaving me with even less space than I had had previously, and I set out for Maine via the Fall River Line. I had come to the conclusion that the less driving I did, the better it would be for my radio. I knew all about connecting it. I knew all there was to be known about tuning it. But unfortunately I knew nothing at all about what made it run, and it was obvious that if something went wrong with it, I would be in a fix.

Which is exactly what happened. I drove up to Maine from Fall River at what, even in those days, was a snail's pace. I checked into the Poland Springs Hotel, which I had chosen as my first port of call. Three bellboys and I took my carful of equipment and set it up in the hotel ballroom. I busied myself connecting batteries and loop aerials and Magnavox speakers and battery chargers, playing to a completely engrossed audience. But when I finally turned the set on and tried to tune in a station, all I could get was absolute dead silence. I took things apart and tried to trace wiring and find possible broken parts. No success. I called on all available local talent with no better luck. Finally I wired New York for another set to be sent up by express as quickly as possible. In the meantime I tried to make myself believe that an innkeeper would actually invest money in something that was so obviously temperamental. I didn't quite manage to do it, but I came sufficiently close to be able to enjoy the days I spent waiting for the other set to arrive.

That was about six days later. The three bellboys and I carted it up from the nearest station, and again I went through my involved act. My audience this time was quite obviously much more skeptical and seemed to expect the final result I achieved—a result that in no way differed from what I had been able to manage with the other set. It was obvious that something was very wrong, and it was equally obvious that I was not the person to solve the problem. I suddenly had visions of myself going through this same experience in hotel after hotel, with set after set coming on from New York. I checked out of the hotel as quickly as I could, leaving all my equipment and both sets sitting in the ballroom. I have often wondered what happened to it all.

Back in New York I sold the car, paid for the second set, and headed for Philadelphia and my job as a boilermaker in the Baldwin Locomotive Works. I had paid the penalty of being ten years ahead of time.

After a while I became fairly adept with the simpler sets. I actually built one at one point, and it worked pretty well. I knew how to coax the maximum of distance out of any set I had. Havana was a local station as far as I was concerned, and I could count on getting the Coast at least twice a week. But I still did not bother to listen to what was coming over the air. The station announcement was all I cared about, so that I could make another notation in the little notebook I kept for the purpose. It wasn't until some years later that I began to take some interest in tone and in the programs that were being broadcast. And then I filled my apartment with battery eliminators that made a humming sound slightly different from battery chargers; with huge cone-shaped paper speakers that reacted instantaneously to changes in humidity and drooped disconsolately in rainy weather; and with a series of radios that came in and out as new circuits appeared and were briefly publicized. The only set I kept for any length of time was a Grebe Neutrodyne, a fine set that gave me all I wanted from a radio. But it did have one great drawback. It was operated by three major controls of equal importance, and it presupposed that the user had three hands. Handicapped as I was by having one short of that number, I would take many minutes getting all three dials lined up properly. And even if I did finally succeed in doing this, there was still the problem of compensating for the extra volume I would get as I approached the set. In those days a radio was as definitely a one-man proposition as any dog. You had to know your set as well as you would your animal if you did not want to get the same noise from it that you would by stepping on your puppy's tail.

But my ultimate humiliation in radio was still many years ahead of me. In 1942 I was sent to the Air Corps Radio School in Sioux Falls. I took it very seriously, and I found that my experience with radios stood me in very good stead. I had no trouble at all in assembling the sets that were used for our primary training, and in absorbing the information that was pushed at us with the speed of a conveyor belt gone mad. I had visions of myself in a plane doing Mittylike deeds as a radio operator. And then gradually I began to realize something. While I was doing exceedingly well in my technical studies, I was finding it absolutely impossible to learn code. After six weeks of studying for three to four hours a day, I was still among the dunces, those poor souls who could not yet transcribe even ten words a minute. My classmates were most of them in the thirty-word-a-minute group, and some of them were doing even better than that. My transfer came just in time. If it had not come when it did, I would have had to put in two hours a night practicing code, trying to prove to the authorities that I was not a moron. And somehow I have the feeling that I would never have succeeded—even with the expert testimony of the grocer from Sharon, Connecticut.

MATINEES
WEDNESDAYS
AND
SATURDAYS

$\mathcal{T}$HE theater, of course, was something else again. Radio was to be developed to its present point of technical perfection in my lifetime, but this period was also to see the steady decline of the stage to its present sorry state. I'm glad I managed to crowd all of it I could into my early years. As a result I have some wonderful memories of never-to-be-repeated moments.

I managed to start when I was pretty young. In Moscow I went to the opera house a great deal, and I heard Chaliapin often, and a tenor, Sobinoff, who was held to be Caruso's equal, and beautiful performances of all the classic operas sung by singers whose reputations may never have become world-wide but who, nonetheless, were outstanding. But the thing I enjoyed most was the ballet. I went as often as I could. There was one dancer I never tired of watching, and whose miraculous leaping entrances I have never forgotten. It wasn't until many years later that I realized this artist whom I had enjoyed so completely was the young Nijinsky.

There were other great theatrical moments for me: Sarah Bernhardt in *L'Aiglon*, and the Moscow Art Theater, and in St. Petersburg open-air performances of *The Inspector General* and *Twenty Thousand Leagues under the Sea*. These were particularly exciting to a child, played as they were on a stage only slightly smaller than the Hippodrome's, and played broadly for laughs and gasps. And in the Caucasus, where we spent a number of summers, there was open-air opera, which was doubly thrilling because of the snow-covered mountains shining in the moonlight back of the shell.

And then there were circuses in Moscow and in St. Petersburg. These were one-ring circuses in circular houses built especially for them, and the acts were wonderful even though I had usually seen them before in other countries. The finale was always the same though: the ring would sink, water would be pumped in, and boats would come floating in through the various entrances. And on this aquatic note the circus would close, the sawdust floating on top of the dirty water not detracting in the least from the wonderful excitement of the spectacle.

On my early and occasional trips to New York I would go to the Hippodrome itself, that incredible place that has such an important part in the childhood memories of so many people. The last time I was in it was on the opening night of *Jumbo* in 1935 when it had been transformed by Billy Rose into the plushest circus that anyone had ever dreamed of. I don't like to remember it that way. I prefer to think of a block-wide stage covered with tulips, with the huge cast in appropriate costumes singing *When It's Tulip Time in Holland*. Or of the fantastic shows called something like *A Trip to Mars*, with every one of the tricks of which the Hippodrome was capable being brought into play. Or I can evoke memories of Annette Kellerman and the huge tank that came into being on the stage, and the diving girls, and then the elephants, who would disappear into the water before our very eyes, never to be seen again. It was thrilling even if you had been told exactly how it was done. After all, you did not have to believe all you were told.

When I came back to America for good, there were De Wolfe Hopper in *Iolanthe* and Montgomery and Stone in *The Red Mill* and my first real musical comedy, *Leave It to Jane*. And after that came the deluge.

In the twenties an average of some two hundred shows each year opened on Broadway. I did not see them all, but I did my best, and there were some wonderful moments to remember, starting with the out-of-town tryouts while I was at college. There was the night in New Haven when one of the clubs had reserved all the seats on either side of the runway for the opening of a new Winter Garden show, and on a given signal every man along the entire length of this ramp had climbed up on it and got into the act, dancing with the girls, kissing them, raising hell generally. The police had been called to stop the riot, and the runway had been torn out the following night so that there could be no recurrence of this catastrophe. And at Princeton there had been the trips to Philadelphia to see *The Night Boat* as often as possible in its pre-Broadway run, and week ends in New York jammed with as many plays as we could possibly get to see, invariably ending up with hours spent at Justine Johnson's feet at the Little Club.

And then there were the wonderful intimate musicals by the team of Wodehouse and Bolton and Kern, and the *Follies* and the *Midnight Frolics* and the shows on the Century Roof. And there was *Sally*—which I saw twenty-seven times.

I suppose it would be more correct to say that I saw Marilyn Miller in it twenty-seven times. I had met her on the *Paris* coming back from Europe in 1920. She was almost as young as I was, and even though she had been in a number of Ziegfeld shows, she was still comparatively unknown. She was returning to America to begin rehearsals for her first starring part, and I became completely devoted to her. I would go to the rehearsals with her, and sit and worship her in the empty theater. And I lived, dreamed, breathed thoughts of the opening night and of taking her out after her triumph. I am sure that I visualized myself pulling her carriage single-handed through the streets. It did not work out quite that way. The first time we went out together, during the early stages of the rehearsals of *Sally*, I took her to the Montmartre, my first visit to that most popular of night clubs without the sponsorship of my older brother. And Charlie Journal, the greatest rope wielder who ever separated the goats from the sheep, would not let us in. I think Marilyn was disappointed in me, although she did not show it. But I did not see her quite so often after this, and as the opening night approached, I grew aware of the fact that she was becoming much too important a person to devote as much time to me as she had. I sat in the Miller family box that night, I went backstage to congratulate her on her triumph, and I watched her prepare to go out with somebody else. And that was the end of my one and only stage-door romance.

But I knew the show by heart by then, and I kept coming back to see it and Marilyn. As I said, I saw it twenty-seven times. And that does not include the times I came in between acts of other shows to stand in the back of the theater and catch a number or two. The doorman knew me well, and he would always let me in.

If I had been stage-struck before, I was doubly so now. No evening was really complete without the obligatory two and a half hours spent in an overheated theater, living the make-believe life that was offered me from the stage. I would have an early dinner and then get a taxi, and we would charge into that most chaotic of messes, the theater-time traffic. It was pretty terrible in those days. One-way streets had not been established, and it was merely a question of bulling your way through a milling crowd of taxicabs, all eager to deposit their customers at the same moment at the dozens of theaters in the basically small theatrical district. Forty-second Street was particularly bad. The best theaters in town were on this street, and most of them housed the hits that everybody wanted to see. It was wisest to allow plenty of time to get there if you didn't want to miss too much of the show.

I rarely missed a moment. I tried to be in my seat well before the lights dimmed and the curtain rose. And somehow I usually managed to make it. The same was true in Philadelphia, where I saw all the shows I could while I was learning to be a locomotive salesman at the Baldwin works. That took even more doing. The job of getting the factory grime off my body took a full half-hour at best, but that was only half the story. There was also the problem of getting into the solitary bathroom in the boarding house where I lived. That could easily take another hour. And then there was the sprint for the station and the local to town, and the taxi to the theater there. Dinner was out of the question: I ate after the show. Somehow I never seemed to think about food while I was in the theater.

It is very different now. Of course I realize that I am older and that escape is not so important to me any more. And I am naturally more set in my habits, and the idea of rushing for anything does not have the same appeal for me that it did. And a good leisurely dinner has become one of the most completely soul-satisfying things I can imagine. But if I were a young man today, I doubt if I would be as theater-hungry as I was in the twenties. It isn't the same theater any more. It has become a proving ground for Hollywood, and the stage itself is nothing more than an auction hall with an asbestos curtain. There are, of course, exceptions to this sweeping statement. The point is that in the twenties these exceptions were the rule.

Take *The Jest* for instance. There was the theater at its most glamorous and exciting, a play of color and movement and swashbuckling excitement, with a cast that romped through it riotously and with the greatest of good humour. Who of us who saw it will ever forget John Barrymore's entrance when he stood posed on the castle steps, resplendent in tights, probably as fully aware of the sighs of the women in the audience as we were? He was out to make his name in this play, and he had told a friend that he planned to use every trick of acting that had ever been used before, and every one he could devise as well, to make the critics and the audience hail him as America's greatest actor. It worked too. When he did *Hamlet* a short time later, the critics fell all over themselves in rapture. And so did the audiences, myself included.

Today one production like that would make a Broadway season. Then you had your pick of a dozen, and they were as varied as they were good. There was, for instance, George Arliss, the prototype of cynical evil in his elaborate costume, gliding with magnificent skill through that most competent of all melodramas, *The Green Goddess*. Or Ed Wynn, cackling like a happy hen, the zany to end all zanies, playing himself in *The Perfect Fool*. It was in that show, or in any case in one of his very early ones, that he demonstrated his immortal invention the perfected corn-on-the-cob server, a simple device that required only a stripped typewriter, whose carriage held the dripping ear of corn, with the tinkling bell informing the diner that he had come to the end of a row. We rolled in the aisles at this one. We did the same for Balieff and his carefully practiced broken English when the *Chauve Souris* came to town. And we reacted as we had been expected to when the whole of the theater during a performance of the *Music Box Revue* suddenly filled with orange-blossom perfume to give an additional dimension to our enjoyment of the song that was one of the features of the show, a Hippodromesque item entitled *An Orange Grove in California*.

And that is just part of the picture. In those days the Theatre Guild was still considered way downtown, and Shaw and O'Neill were its own particular property. I never missed any of their productions at the Garrick Theater, even if it meant, as it did in the case of *Back to Methuselah*, coming back to this theater for three consecutive Wednesdays.

And the same was true of the Moscow Art Theater and their magnificent season of repertory. And later there were the Neighborhood Playhouse and some of the most exciting and amusing moments I have ever known in the theater. There were the last of the great Belasco productions too; and *R.U.R.*; and Helen Hayes in *Cæsar and Cleopatra*; and Louis Wolheim in *What Price Glory?*; and Katharine Cornell in *The Green Hat* and *Outward Bound*, which I saw on its opening night in Philadelphia, when the first-act curtain came as a shattering shock to the entire audience; and Jeanne Eagels in *Rain*, which I saw there too before her triumphant arrival in New York. And there were the Charlot reviews with Beatrice Lillie and Gertrude Lawrence and Jack Buchanan, and the Joe Cook musicals, and the Four Marx Brothers, and W. C. Fields, and hours of marvelous vaudeville at the Palace. It was a golden era, and I made the most of it.

There was, inevitably, some dross in the gold. The first fifteen minutes of *Abie's Irish Rose*, for instance, seen in Atlantic City for want of anything else to see, and walked out on without hesitation as quickly as possible. And the incredible spectacle of *The Miracle*, with the whole of the Century Theater rebuilt to resemble a cathedral, the only thing spoiling the otherwise magnificent effect being the atrocious acoustics, which gave you first the sounds from the stage, and a split second later their echo from the rear of the theater. But these occasional fiascoes were to be expected. The law of averages took care of that.

And then there was the opera, with Farrar and Scotti and Jeritza and Gigli and Titta Ruffo—and Caruso. I was at the Metropolitan the night he sang in *Samson and Delilah*, and something went wrong when he pulled the temple down on him, and they rang down the curtain and tried to ease his bruised chest. It was the beginning of the end for him, and opera somehow never seemed quite the same to me after he died.

There were also, of course, movies. In Russia I had seen Max Linder comedies, and long, overacted versions of *Les Miserables*, and I had sneaked off to see bedroom farces that were popular with the masses and that left very little to your imagination. Back in America I had gone to the outdoor theaters that showed Chaplin shorts and John Bunny comedies. At college I had gone to pictures often, as a method of using up the time that hung heavy on my hands, and had listened to and joined in with the steady stream of jokes and comments that accompanied the showing of a picture in the Princeton theater. And there had been the time I was trying to be a bond salesman when, disgusted with my lack of success in my work, I would spend hours in a theater in the financial district which opened at nine in the morning for just such unhappy creatures as myself.

But I did not go to pictures often in the following years. I saw all the Chaplin and Keaton and Lloyd pictures, and Fatty Arbuckle in *Brewster's Millions*, and the Douglas Fairbanks films. Later there were *Caligari* and *The Golem* and all the other pictures made in Germany, and the sophisticated pictures that Von Stroheim made so beautifully, and the simple tear jerkers produced by Griffith, and the first animated cartoons. Still later there were the abstract *avant-garde* films, which I thought of as a new form of art rather than as movies. And that was about all. There was much too much to see in the theater for me to waste my time on films.

And there was also much too much going on in the world of sports.

SIXTEEN

A
RINGSIDE
SEAT

Sᴘᴏʀᴛs were an important part of our
lives in the twenties. Spectator sports, I mean. Outside of
a bit of tennis and a little bit more golf, we were much
too busy watching others compete ever to do any of it ourselves. Skiing was still something that you had to go to
Switzerland to do: the cult of the healthy mind in the
chilled body was as yet very much in the future.

But as spectators we had an infinite variety of choice.
In its farthest reaches it included such things as marathon
dancing, flagpole sitting, a transcontinental foot race, and
the receptions given to returning Channel swimmers. But
on the more familiar levels it offered fully as much variety.
And we sampled all the forms eagerly.

I got my start in big-league sport quite early in my life.
I was just twenty when I saw the Dempsey-Carpentier
fight in the wooden reaches of Boyle's Thirty Acres in the
New Jersey flat lands. My brother and I shared a box with
Big Bill Edwards, which was quite a feat in itself in view
of his colossal bulk. And it was in connection with this
fight that I had my first heady taste of the pleasures of
privilege. For some reason I have forgotten, my brother

had been issued a police-department license by the city authorities, and I had enjoyed the experience of driving in the city with him, watching the cops stop all traffic in order to let us continue on our way, saluting smartly as we drove past. It had been my duty to answer their salutes, since the driver obviously had both his hands occupied.

But when we started for the ferry that was to take us to New Jersey and the fight, we had no idea of whether or not the police at the entrances to the ferry slip would recognize the validity of our "PD" license. For one thing, there were by that time so many of these licenses in town that they could easily pre-empt a whole series of ferries for their own use. For another, there was the fact that we were obviously going to New Jersey to see the fight, and that could hardly come under the head of official business for which we were entitled to clearance. In any case we got to the long line waiting to get on the overcrowded ferries, still wondering if we would have to wait our turn at the end of the thousand cars.

We did not. The policeman at the end waved us on to the man ahead of him, as did the next officer and the next one. We drove majestically to the head of the line, trying to ignore the looks of pure hatred thrown at us by the occupants of the cars we passed along the way—all of us except my brother, who was driving, answering the salutes the harried policemen felt obligated to give us. And only when we were safely on the ferry was the rest of the line permitted to move forward.

The result of this break was that we arrived at the stadium much earlier than we had expected to, so early, as a matter of fact, that as we were walking leisurely toward the building, we witnessed the arrival of a tall thin man, completely surrounded by policemen who were clearing the way for him. It was Carpentier arriving for the slaughter, and he seemed to know what was in store for him. I shall never forget his face, dead white, a frozen mask of nervous apprehension. And of course he was right in feeling as he did: he did not belong in the same ring with Dempsey, and he knew it. The fight itself was an anticlimax. Dempsey could have ended it with one punch, and everybody in the stadium was aware of this fact a minute after the bell rang for the first round. We in the box, remembering Carpentier's face, could get little pleasure out of watching Dempsey play with him.

My next big fight was an utterly different thing. It was, as a matter of fact, the greatest fight I ever saw, and maybe even the greatest fight anybody ever saw. It was the Dempsey-Firpo bout at the Polo Grounds, and even though there was no question of privilege involved, we still managed to get a break that enabled us actually to see everything that happened in those frantic five minutes. And that was more than any of the holders of the thousand of ringside seats could say, that is if their seats were any farther back than the first two rows.

Again we had a box, and when we saw where it was, we were annoyed. It was directly back of the visitors' dugout on the third-base side of the field. Ushers and vendors and all manner of people kept popping out from the dugout or congregating in front of it. This is going to be terrible, we told ourselves; we're not going to be able to see anything that goes on in the ring.

Firpo was down for the first time a matter of seconds after the first round started. And we were up, standing on top of the dugout, surrounded by ushers and hot-dog salesmen and the occupants of the adjoining boxes. They all clambered up on the raised platform at the same time, and they stayed there until the fight was over, with Firpo stretched out on the ring floor fifty-seven seconds after the second round began. And we stayed there too. It was tough for us at that: the roof of the dugout was crowded to the last inch of space, and we all had to hang on to each other to keep from being pushed over the edge. But we did not miss one second of the fight. It was only when it was all over and the inevitable reaction set in that we realized how precariously we had been perched. Actually it was some time before this reaction set in. In the taxi on the way downtown we were all still too completely excited to say a word.

My final big fight was the first Dempsey-Tunney fight in Philadelphia. The main problem here was one of logistics, since there was not only the trip to Philadelphia to be considered, but also the problem of how over one hundred thousand people could get from the station to the stadium and then back again to the station, with all of them wanting to move in the same direction at the same time. The first part of this problem was solved quite easily. I went on the special train that had been chartered by the Harvard Club, and it was a rowdy trip both ways—particularly on the way back when we were all soaked to the skin after almost an hour and a half in the rain. But at least we were better off than the poor millionaire who had come on from Chicago in his private car, and who stood in the station after the fight, one short breath this side of apoplexy, while the station master told him apologetically that his car, which had been attached by mistake to a Florida-bound train, would be brought back to Philadelphia just as soon as they could flag down the train and detach the car. It should be back in the station, he was assured, within the next twelve hours.

But the trip to the outer reaches of Philadelphia, where the stadium had been built; and the slow but relentless rain that fell all during the fight; and the mud we sloshed through to try to get a taxi to the station; and the final walk almost all the way across town—these are the things I remember most clearly about this event. The fight itself was pretty dull, especially since Dempsey lost. That was something that we simply could not believe. He had become a symbol of invincibility, like Tilden or Bobby Jones. It would be different, we assured ourselves, when they met again. Dempsey would knock Tunney's block off then.

The big fights were only part of the picture. For a number of years I had a standing reservation for ringside seats to the weekly fights at the Pioneer Athletic Club on West Twenty-fifth Street in New York. And ringside here really meant ringside. More often than not we would leave the place with both blood and water spots on our clothes. If our seats had been any closer we would have been right in the ring with the fighters—and that would not have been too unsafe, for there appeared in the ring in the years in which I attended these fights just about the greatest collection of eager but inept young boxers that have ever been assembled under one roof. They missed ten punches for every one they landed. And when they missed they really did it wholeheartedly: I have often seen them swing themselves completely out of the ring—and into our laps.

The fights took place in a hall that for the rest of the week was a horse-auction house. There was no mistaking this fact. The minute you entered the place it became obvious that there had been horses in it lately, and probably a great number of them at that. And if you happened to lack a sense of smell, you had but to look at the sign that was permanently painted on the side of the balcony. "No guaranty with any horse sold for less than ten dollars," it said. It has always remained my favorite sign.

While most of the fighters were really bad, there were a very few who were more than just promising, and there was one lightweight who seemed destined to become a champion. He was probably the most graceful fighter I have ever seen. Constantly on his toes, he was on the move every second he was in the ring. Nobody seemed to be able to land as much as one single blow on him. And while his opponent wore himself out flailing at thin air, this lightweight—his name was Ruby Goldstein—would be chopping him to pieces with a rapierlike left jab. He would land this punch dozens of times in succession, his right hand cocked for the finishing blow he rarely had to deliver, for as often as not his opponent, cut and bleeding and barely able to stagger, would finally go down under one of the hundreds of left jabs he had taken, and Goldstein would have added another victim to his ever growing list.

In all the times that I saw him fight, I never saw him in trouble once. But I am glad that I did not see his fight with the rough and tough Ace Hudkins at Coney Island. He started off as he always did, and soon had Hudkins completely bewildered. He followed up his advantage relentlessly, and down Hudkins went. So far the fight had gone exactly as all Goldstein's fights always went, and he stepped back to listen to the count. Mentally he was probably already unlacing his gloves and collecting his share of the gate. What happened next was definitely not according to schedule. Hudkins got up. Not only did he get up but he came back fighting. The first punch he threw caught Ruby full on the jaw, and down Goldstein went, completely out, on the canvas for the first time in his life. He had to be carried to his corner, and he never won a major fight after that. I'm glad I was not there. I would have hated to see the look on Goldstein's face when he first became aware of the fact that it was not only possible for a man whom he had knocked down to get up again, but that it was also possible that he himself could be hit and floored.

But prize fights were just one of the attractions offered us. There was international polo, magnificently played on beautiful horses in the pleasantest setting imaginable. It didn't matter too much if you did not understand all the subtleties of the game. Most of the people around you did

not understand them either. There was top-flight tennis at
Forest Hills, with Tilden and Johnston and Vincent Rich-
ards, and later Borotra and Lacoste, who unbelievably
managed to defeat them. And there were Babe Ruth and
the Yankees—I sat way up in the top balcony for the opening game in the Yankee Stadium, eager to be part of the
tremendous crowd that filled every inch of the place—and
the time Ruth caught a fly backed up against the right-
field wall, and caught the man coming home from third
after the catch with the most incredibly perfect throw I
have ever seen. And there was football.

If any one sport was outstanding in the twenties, it was
football. There were many reasons for this. The game had
not yet become so complicated that only the experts, sitting
up in broadcasting booths on the top of the stadium, had
any idea of what was going on on the field. A trick play
was very definitely the exception. I can clearly remember
one of the very few I saw in those years. It was in a Yale-
Princeton game, and it won the game for Princeton. And
all that happened was that the Princeton quarterback,
Jack Strubing, dropped back as if to try for a place kick.
A teammate took the pass from center and held the ball
down as if for his kick. Strubing waited until the entire
Yale team started in toward him to block the kick, and
then he took the ball from his teammate and ran for a
touchdown. This play was discussed for years. It was held
to be the height of brilliant football. It wouldn't work in a
high-school game today.

There was another thing about football which made it
particularly popular. It was an excellent excuse for drinking. The long ride by train or by car, the cool autumn
weather, the reaction that inevitably set in after the excitement of the game—all these made it essential that there
should be an ample supply of liquor along. As often as not
it was gin. Sometimes it was whisky. But whichever it was,

the container was always the same, a silver flask carried in the hip pocket. After a few hours the liquor would be at body temperature, nasty and gagging. Somehow that didn't seem to matter.

But the thing that probably contributed most to football's popularity was the difficulty in getting tickets. I was particularly fortunate in that I got ticket applications from both Yale and Princeton, and I was always well supplied with tickets for all the games I wanted to see. But since the big stadiums were always sold out for the big games, there were many who could not get in. That only whetted their appetite. It became a point of honor with them to get tickets by hook or crook. There were some pretty nasty scandals each year, and some poor sophomore would find himself socially ostracized simply because he had had the bad fortune to be caught selling his tickets.

I saw practically every major Big Three game played in those years. And Big Three football was considered the only football worth seeing. There was as yet nothing comparable to present-day professional football. Still, the one professional game I saw was to mark the beginning of an entirely new era in the game. It was the first New York appearance of Red Grange as a professional, two weeks after he had played his last game for Illinois. It drew a capacity crowd at the Polo Grounds. I can still remember his magnificent run for a touchdown inches in from the sidelines, with would-be tacklers tumbling in his tracks. His teammates were not exactly fond of him or of the inordinate publicity he was getting. And publicity, not interference, was what he got in this game.

But the one sport that took precedence over all others was drinking. And drinking in the twenties was really a sporting proposition. It involved passwords and travel and smuggling and the constant danger of blindness or worse. For some of us it became a career in itself.

SEVENTEEN

AS THE
ELBOW
IS
BENT

I WAS barely eight years old when I had my first drink of hard liquor: a hefty slug of vodka that my father gave me in a vain attempt to ward off an attack of seasickness. The place was a converted icebreaker, and the occasion a trip from St. Petersburg to Kronstadt to greet the American battleships that were stopping there on their round-the-world cruise. The entire American colony was on board and, as I remember it, they were all seasick, from the ambassador on down.

My second unfortunate experience with drinking was also connected with the American ambassador to Russia. The place was Moscow, and the occasion a dinner Father gave for that august character. But it was not vodka that was my downfall this time; it was a beautiful bottle of champagne—Louis Roederer Brut, and probably 1906— and I shall always remember it with pleasure. I was thirteen years old, and I was permitted to say good night to our guests before retiring to my room for the night. But I had taken the precaution of putting a well-chilled bottle in my room before the company arrived, and I spent a deliciously quiet evening there, savoring the wonderful wine slowly and completely. The fact that I was more than slightly hung over the following morning might have been attributed to the cold that I claimed had it not been that I was caught trying to return the empty champagne bottle to the pantry. The punishment that was given me fitted the crime I had committed, but I did not care; I had had my pleasure and was quite willing to pay for it.

And then there was the time, a little earlier, when we went through the Czar's private cellars in the Crimea and I sampled so many sweet wines that I have never been able to look at a glass of even the finest of Tokays since then.

Actually I was permitted fairly liberal amounts of wine from my very early childhood. We traveled constantly, and it was a well-known fact that water was a drink to be shunned unless it was carefully boiled first. And boiled water is just about the dullest and least thirst-quenching drink in the world. So I was permitted to add wine to my water, and then to drink a glass or so of wine with my meals. And on the seemingly continuous train trips we took, there was always the glass of beer at the station restaurant. And for special occasions there was champagne. There was champagne too on especially rough ocean crossings, or a small glass of excellent brandy if the storm, as was often the case, proved to be of almost typhoonlike intensity. I was very definitely not brought up to be a teetotaler.

It was not, however, until I broke away from parental supervision, in my freshman year at Yale in 1919, that I first began to experiment with hard liquors. I made up for lost time then. I fancied myself a great tosspot, and I would drink endlessly at the many cafés in town or at the Taft Bar. As I remember it, I carried my liquor well most of the time, and I can still boast that during the long years of Prohibition there never was one occasion in which I was not completely aware of exactly what I was doing. I did, however, come very close to spoiling that record early in my drinking career. That was the time I bet some friends at the Taft Bar that I could drink ten straight Scotches within half an hour, walk home to my rooms some six blocks away, and then walk a straight line in my rooms half an hour after I had downed the tenth drink. I made it—but just barely. I did not get much enjoyment out of the money I won.

I was at Princeton when Prohibition came in, and I went up to New York for that fantastic evening. As a matter of fact I spent most of the evening at Reisenweber's, and I carried home a bottle of the excellent liquor given away that night under the honest impression that there would never again be any selling or drinking of liquor in America. It didn't matter very much to me at that point. I had passed through the difficult stage, and while I enjoyed drinking I did not enjoy it enough to realize how much I would miss it. I patronized the early speakeasies in Princeton hardly at all. I did not relish drinking cheap liquor out of heavy glass tumblers in a dirty kitchen. And in the following summer, when raw alcohol mixed with any kind of fruit juice was almost the national drink, I enjoyed it even less. It wasn't until things got very much better organized that I began my adult drinking.

It was very soon discovered that gin was the easiest liquor to produce. All you needed was good alcohol and some juniper extract and a large enough container in which to mix these simple ingredients. It was not until some time later that the great discovery was made that a bathtub was ideally suited for mixing purposes. In any case the first bootlegging drugstore I can remember was on Seventh Avenue, right next door to the Al Jolson Theater, and its specialty was gin and gin only. You were introduced to the manager by one of the regular patrons, and you signed your name in a big book that was kept at the back of the store. After that, whenever you wanted a bottle of gin you signed your name on a slip of paper, and this signature was compared with the one in the book. After they had made an increasingly cursory glance to verify the legitimacy of your signature, you paid your two dollars and walked out with a pint bottle on your hip.

It was very shortly after this that the first real speak-easy in New York opened for business. It was on Forty-fifth Street near Fifth Avenue, and you walked through an absolutely deserted restaurant to some curtained stairs in the rear. At the foot of these stairs there was a locked door with a peephole, and if you were recognized, you soon found yourself sitting in a broken-down wicker chair in a stuffy basement, while the drink you had ordered was served to you in a chipped coffee cup. You could order almost anything you wanted there, but the favorite drink at the time was an atrocity called an Orange Blossom, made of equal parts of orange juice and of gin, and reminding me forcefully of early experiences with castor oil.

This place, which was running full blast by the summer of 1922, was the forerunner of innumerable similar joints, all stuffy and shabby and openly furtive. It was not until two or three years later that the acceptable scale for police protection was worked out and things finally came to the point where a respectable householder on Fifty-second Street put up a sign reading: "This is a Private House," to discourage the constant stream of visitors who were certain that every house on that block was a speakeasy. And then came the deluge of speakeasy cards, as essential in those days as the draft card many years later. And the peepholes and the chain-locked doors, and the bars running full blast, and the excellent food that many of these places served—

214

all these things were to be a natural part of our life for the next ten years.

I was extremely fortunate in that I knew very little about most of them. My father had had the foresight to buy up the cellar of one of New York's leading hotels just before Prohibition became the law of the land. After his death the following year, while we were living in small apartments rather than in the large country house where he had planned to lay down the really magnificent collection he had acquired, the hundreds of cases of liquor were stored in the garage of a cousin's house in the country. When I finally moved into my own apartment in 1924 my brother and I decided to divide the cellar between us. It was only then that we discovered that fully half of the cases had disappeared. And the thieves, whoever they were, certainly had excellent taste in liquor: all of the wonderful bottled-in-bond bourbon and most of the fine Scotches had been taken, as had dozens of cases of fine brandies. But what was left was still worth its weight in gold, and we were grateful for it. We did not finish the last of our bottles until late in 1926.

With this cellar as a backlog I would have been foolish to patronize the local speakeasies with their questionable liquor. Naturally I did not stay at home night after night drinking my fine wines as a miser would count his gold. But I did far less public drinking than a great number of my contemporaries, and most of it was at Italian or French speakeasies, where the food was excellent and a good bottle of wine was almost *de rigueur*. And I had in the meantime made an important discovery.

It was Ernest Boyd who told me about it. This bearded man about town was as fine a two-fisted drinker as I had ever met. I cannot remember ever seeing him without a glass in his hand. And all that the glass ever contained was Irish whisky and soda. He told me why one day. For one thing, he said, he liked it better than any other drink. For another he had figured out that there was such a small demand for Irish whisky that it was not worth while for the bootleggers to go to the trouble of cutting it or of imitating it. What little they smuggled in could be sold easily to their regular customers. This seemed to make a great deal of sense to me, so much, as a matter of fact, that Irish was practically all I would drink from then on. And for some time after that, it continued to be comparatively easy to get. When smuggling activities were clamped down on a few years later, and the trickle of Irish that had come into the country dried up, I took a step that was pretty daring in those days: I went on the wagon, probably the most arrogantly ostentatious move I could have made, and I stayed there for two years, until the flow of good liquor was finally resumed.

There was one speakeasy I did patronize a great deal: Tony's on West Fifty-second Street. It was the literary rendezvous of the period, and it was rowdy and amusing and always filled with all the writers and actors and critics whom you wanted to see. It was an unpretentious place, with wooden tables scarred with hundreds of initials that had been carved in them by hundreds of patrons. And Tony was the perfect host for the difficult people he had to deal with. He never seemed to have any difficulty in handling the clashing temperaments that made for an atmosphere constantly charged with electricity. I was there at least three nights a week for many years. I was never bored.

There were, of course, many other places. There were Mori's and Barney Gallant's in the Village, and downtown in the shadow of City Hall there was Moneta's. All of these places served excellent food and good wine, and I went to them often. And there was Jack and Charlie's, which was an occasional place for me, and which I did not start to patronize until many years later, after I had taken root in Hollywood. And uptown in Harlem there was Small's, where the music and the floor show were wonderful, and the liquor was so new that you prayed for the best as you drank it.

And there were the plush night clubs, where I never went at all. I never set foot in any of Texas Guinan's various establishments or in the dozens of places operated by her imitators. My occasional night clubbing was limited to going to the Montmartre or the Palais Royal in its Paul Whiteman days; to watching the fantastically graceful Maurice make mock of all his partners no matter how good they happened to be; to listening night after night to Florence Mills at the Plantation. And then for a short while there was the Jungle Room with its deserted front room and jammed bar. But that was one of the few exceptions to my rule about night clubs where I had to rely on the liquor a waiter would slip me surreptitiously, or drink the house equivalent of the Scotch-and-soda I had ordered. I preferred the places where I could bring my own flask and drink my own liquor, safe in the knowledge that I was downing something I could vouch for.

The only drinking I really enjoyed in those years was on shipboard or in Europe. It was a wonderful feeling to know that you were getting exactly what you ordered, and that your next drink would be quite as good as the one you were savoring so gratefully now that the ship's bar had finally opened. There was no hurry. You didn't have to try to drink up all the liquor in the bottle simply because the next bottle might be terrible. You could relax.

That was particularly true on transatlantic crossings. One of the main reasons for this was that strange institution the midnight sailing, and the inevitable farewell parties in a crowded stateroom, with the guests, invited and not, making a shambles of the cabin. The stewards were as accommodating as they dared to be, and it was not too difficult to arrange for a supply of champagne and Scotch with which to set up a makeshift bar on the bed. One thing you never had to worry about: the problem of disposing of unconsumed liquor never arose. When the final "All visitors ashore" had been called up and down the passageways, there would be a frantic cramming of bottles into pockets, and a careful draping of clothes in such a way as to disguise the resultant bulges. And your friends, many of them hardly able to negotiate the long gangplank, would stagger past the guards at the gate, completely intent on achieving their one purpose of sneaking a bottle of real liquor off the dock. After a while the guards were instructed to run their hands lightly over the clothes of the departing multitudes, and for a time while this rule was enforced there was an astonishing dropping off of the well-wishing friends who seemed to think of you only in relation to those magical words "Sails one minute after midnight, Saturday morning."

But with the cabin emptied of guests, even though the empty bottles and glasses and full ash trays remained to remind you of their solicitude, there still remained one problem that you could only hope you had protected yourself against effectively enough. That was the device used by the racketeering bootleggers to get rid of untold cases of seemingly genuine bottles all neatly filled to the top with cold tea. Their method was simplicity itself. They would study the sailing lists, and very early in the morning, after you were safely out at sea, they would call your secretary on the telephone. They would introduce themselves as friends of a steward on the liner on which you had sailed, and they would tell the secretary that you had made arrangements for them to deliver one, two, three cases, as many as they felt the traffic would bear, of guaranteed straight-off-the-ship whisky at so and so much per case. When, they would ask, would the secretary like them to deliver the liquor? And would she mind paying them in cash for it? Obviously they could not accept checks.

And the poor secretary, if she had not been warned against this gag, would really find herself in a spot. If you had indeed ordered the liquor and she did not accept delivery of it and pay for it, you would be furious when you got back. She could hardly wireless you and ask you if you had conspired to violate the law. As often as not, therefore, she would accept the cases, which were brought to your office by a very seagoing man. And when you came back, you would find that you were out a great deal of money and in a fine collection of cold tea.

But if you had guarded against this happening to you, as you probably had if you were not making your first crossing, you were still faced with disposing of the gifts your friends had sent you to the ship. It was fashionable to try very hard to be funny in choosing the presents you sent to your departing friends, and I once received a case of particularly bad bootleg liquor, which was ceremoniously wheeled into my cabin on the *Paris* right after the ship had sailed, to tease me for my obvious delight at leaving my "dry" homeland. Disposing of it proved to be quite a problem. I finally solved it by emptying all twelve bottles into the Atlantic and tossing the empty bottles after the liquor. But my brother was once faced with a more difficult problem: he found a pair of rabbits in one of the boxes that were delivered to his cabin the morning after a particularly hectic farewell party. You definitely could not throw live rabbits overboard, and yet he had to dispose of them quickly, for it was certain that there would soon be many more than two rabbits in the box. He managed to get rid of them somehow, but it must have taken quite a bit of figuring out.

With all these hazards back of you, it was finally possible to begin enjoying yourself. And, except for the very small minority that reacted to an open bar as a cat does to catnip, the drinking on shipboard was orderly and pleasant, even if somewhat more constant than seemed physically possible. The pleasure of being able to enjoy the taste of what you were drinking was a memorable experience in those days. And if your palate had not been completely anesthetized by corrosive draughts of cut and green and often poisoned liquids, arbitrarily labeled with whatever sticker was handiest, it was an experience you wanted to enjoy to the full. Since I still retained the full faculties of all my taste buds, I managed to have a wonderful time on every trip I took.

This was equally true of cruises, although they posed their own kind of problem. For most people the basic reason for a cruise was to catch up on drinking, and if you were not careful you would find that there would be no time for anything else. The first thing to do, I soon found out, was to get clear of the entire smoking-room crowd and establish yourself in the quiet grillroom, where you could eat and drink in comparative solitude, avoiding the brawls and lusty good-fellowship of the aggressively convivial group above. If you did that, a cruise was fun. If you didn't, you found yourself swept up in an endless stream of Martinis, Daiquiris, and Pink Ladies. And that was not my idea of fun.

The same thing was true of drinking in Europe. I was a Ritz Bar man on and off, and I knew and enjoyed some of the smaller pubs and some of the more exciting night clubs, notably the Casanova and later the Bateau Ivre. But I am as proud of the fact that I was never in Zelli's or Harry's American Bar as I am of the fact that during my whole college career I never once went to the Pre-Catalan in New York. It may be snobbish and affected, but that is the way I feel about it. Drinking for me is for pleasure, and I had around me constantly the visible examples of those who drank for escape. It always seemed like a pretty silly performance, and a not particularly effective one.

But there was one thing which I shared with all my fellow travelers, whether it was on a cruise ship or on an ocean liner. That was the very involved preparations we all started to make, a few days before we were due to arrive in New York, to devise a foolproof method of smuggling a few precious bottles of wine ashore with us. I always claimed that it would be possible to bring in a Jeroboam of champagne quite easily, since I doubted if any customs man would believe that a huge bottle carried openly down the gangplank would be anything but a dummy bought for a souvenir. Unfortunately I never made the actual attempt. But short of that I tried everything else. I hid bottles in my shoes, in my laundry, at the back of trunks, in overcoat pockets. I placed them neatly on top of my shirts in my suitcase, with a five-dollar bill tucked in next to them. And I finally evolved the foolproof solution. The bottles would be in full view in the top tray of my suitcase, and next to them would be my business card. The customs inspector would palm the card deftly, and a few days later he would pay me a visit at my office. And we would have a drink together, and I would give him a ten-dollar bill, and everybody would be happy. In all the times I came in to New York I only had my bottles confiscated once, and that was in my laundry-hiding days. Then I stood miserably on the dock, listening to the sound of bottles being broken, and paying a five dollar fine for every one that was being smashed in front of my eyes. The fact that my wife was by that time safely in a taxi on the way home, burdened down with four bottles of cognac that swung loosely inside her fur coat, the heavy wool golf stockings into which we had stuffed the bottles being fastened by safety pins, did not quite make up for the sight of the fine liquor running down the gutters of the concrete floor of the dock.

In the latter days of Prohibition, things were increasingly simple. It was possible to get all the really good liquor you wanted by simply picking up your telephone at any time of the day or night. It would be delivered to you promptly, and you ran an account with your bootlegger just as naturally as you did with the butcher or the grocer. There were increasingly more restaurants where you could get excellent French wines and more than palatable domestic products. There were also the barrels of grape juice you would buy, and which would bubble away in the kitchen, effectively checked every so often by a man whose services were included in the cost of the grape juice, and who would even take care of the final bottling of your homemade wine for you. I tried this only once, and I liked neither the product nor the strange odor that the barrel gave off in its two months' occupancy of the kitchen. And I never did try the wine bricks that came along shortly after this: they seemed like an impossible oversimplification of the art of wine making. Besides, why go to all this bother? I could get cases of really good wine from Moneta's or from any one of a dozen other places—or I could drink it at any speakeasy I chose to patronize.

The speakeasies too changed considerably as the day of repeal came closer. They were running almost wide open now, and the liquor they served was excellent and only slightly cut. I rarely bothered with a flask anymore except for football games. And even there it was no longer necessary to duck down and take a swig of the hip-warmed liquor as if you were trying to do the most involved kind of acrobatics. Between halves everybody stood around under the stadiums drinking openly and without fear of the consequences. And it was no longer the smart thing to do to get reeling drunk and start a fight in the stands. People looked pityingly on the drunk who had become too obstreperous and whom the police were escorting down the ramp. A few years before, there might easily have been a free-for-all in an attempt to rescue him from the cops.

But there were two memorable moments in these last few years of the great experiment. There was the night I took Clarence Darrow and Arthur Garfield Hays to the Stork Club after a radio broadcast. Darrow was at his best that night, and all of us, Billingsley included, sat in silent fascination listening to him. When we finally left, we were loaded down with bottles of Irish whisky as a token of his esteem and admiration. It was excellent Irish too.

And then there was the night of the raid on Tony's. How he had managed to avoid being raided before, nobody ever knew. But it happened to him finally just a very short time before repeal. When I got out of the cab in front of his place that night, it was obvious that something was wrong. I had never before seen two policemen standing in front of the door. And then I saw Andy, Tony's headwaiter, standing a few doors away and beckoning to me. There's been a raid, he told me. We can't open tonight. But go on up to Twenty-One. That's where they're all going. And when I got there I found Tony at the bar playing host to his regular customers, and all the drinks on the house. It was almost as if Mr. Macy were entertaining Mr. Gimbel —a fitting note for the end of an era.

EIGHTEEN

YOUNG
AESTHETE

On FEBRUARY 12th, 1924, the old Aeolian Hall on Forty-third Street was the scene of a major musical event, the premiere of George Gershwin's *Rhapsody in Blue.*

I was not there. It seems impossible, but the fact remains that I wasn't. However, it was just about the only event that might be termed *avant-garde* that I managed to miss in the course of the next decade. I ran with the pack that ran ahead of those who ran with the pack. Most of the things I did, I did not quite understand. But that did not bother me too much. I was certain that many of my companions did not understand them either.

The basic principle on which we operated, whether we knew it or not, was that if our parents liked anything it could not possibly be good. And, conversely, if they were baffled, angered, or merely bored, then it must be good, and in direct ratio to their unfavorable reactions. Bach, Beethoven, Chopin, Mozart—we dismissed them all with a casual shrug. Stravinsky was our God, and later Henry Cowell and his tone clusters, played with fist and elbow and occasionally even with his ten fingers. I kept wondering, the night he performed for us on my baby piano, if the poor little machine would stand up under his attack. I wondered, but I said nothing about the fact that I was wondering. I did not dare to; it would have stamped me as old-fashioned, maybe even as Victorian. That last was the supreme insult—and to avoid it we would go to any length.

For instance, before we went to a concert, we would always call Carnegie Hall to find out at what time the Stravinsky *Sacre du Printemps* would go on. We would stand out in the lobby smoking until the orchestra had finished playing that old fuddy-duddy Haydn. Then we would troop in, swoon orgiastically over the atonal music we had come to hear, and troop out again, careful to be safely in the lobby before our ears were assailed by the horribly melodic music of Johannes Brahms. Not that Stravinsky's music had necessarily given us any real pleasure. The chances were excellent that we were not sufficiently intelligent to truly appreciate his art. But we had been taught that Haydn and Brahms were masters—and to that word we automatically prefixed another one: "old." To admire them was almost the same as admitting that Rubens was a great painter, which in turn was only one step removed from admiring Maxfield Parrish.

My Matisse was a case in point. It wasn't a very good Matisse and I really did not like it very much, but it made me feel that I had finally and completely broken with my Zorn youth. I hung it on my wall in much the same way as the aesthetes of the Beardsley period wore their sunflowers, and for much the same reasons. But at least it was a Matisse, which was more than I could say for the painting that dominated my office, well centered over the fireplace where it could not be avoided as you came into the room.

The catalogue description of this painting—it was part of the John Quinn collection, and I bought it at the auction that followed his death—is probably the best one of it I can give. "Suggesting a plastic, prismatic view of a lady," it read, "seated at a table, wearing a dark red hat with a brilliant blue osprey, and smoking a cigarette. Upon the table, in geometric abstraction, are a goblet of wine, a fan and box of cigarettes. Strongly portrayed with intense color contrasts." It was called *La Fumeuse* and it was by Jean Metzinger. And I could never decide why I had bought it. I finally came to the conclusion that it was because I had already bought four Marie Laurencins earlier in the sale and needed a change of pace.

Anyway, my wife refused to let me hang it in our house, thereby showing excellent judgment. After a while I got accustomed to it in my office, and was able to sit there for days at a time without being aware of the object on the wall. For those in the firm who really disliked it there was always the simple expedient of not coming to my office but making me go to theirs. When I left Liveright I left *La Fumeuse* where she had been for the previous two years. I have never wondered what became of her.

It was in that period that I entertained at home dressed in black trousers, blue shirt, and black tie, complemented by a blue brocaded lounging jacket that tied around me with a long sash. On my feet I wore light-blue Russian boots that were approximately eighteen inches high. And I smoked Fatimas only—which I bought in vacuum-sealed tins that were intended for the export trade—in a long jade cigarette holder. My wife usually wore a Babani negligee, a creation made of iridescent velvet, tastefully garnished with heavy gold lace at the neck and cuffs. We gave parties to celebrate the unveiling of Ernest Boyd's brown tuxedo, to introduce the Hall Johnson Choir, to welcome the Irma Duncan dancers. It was inevitable that we should feel the need of a Matisse to fill in the background.

The one we finally bought was a small head of a woman

who obviously should have been done away with at birth. She was ugly beyond belief, definitely cross-eyed, and about as unhappy as any female I had ever seen. But she was a genuine hand-painted Matisse, and I paid a great deal of money for her. When I had finally found the proper place on the wall for her, I began to think of myself as a junior Chester Dale. And it was at this point that I also began to think of buying one of Brancusi's *Birds in Flight*.

I had been called as a witness in the case of *C. Brancusi* v. *United States*, which arose out of the decision by the collector of customs that this was obviously a case where it was the intention of the importer to avoid paying duty on a massive lump of bronze by casting it in an unusual form and claiming that it was a work of art. "The importation," he said, "appears to be a production in bronze about $4\frac{1}{2}$ feet high supported by a cylindrical base about 6 inches in diameter and 6 inches high. It is highly polished, symmetrically constructed, and terminates at the top in a point. It increases in size as it descends with a slight curve to the middle from which point it decreases and terminates about 10 inches from the pedestal where it is cylindrical, and from that point it increases in size in a conical shaped base which rests upon the pedestal." The duty on this piece of metal, he announced, would be forty per cent ad valorem.

The decision was of course immediately appealed, and I found myself involved because of the fact that I was at that time negotiating with Brancusi for a duplicate of this sculpture. I had been taken to his studio in Paris the previous summer, and I had been moved as I had rarely been moved before by my first view of this shining column, displayed against a piece of faded blue velvet, the sun that streamed on it from the studio skylight making it seem to be floating in space, away from clutching hands or mortal view. Then and there I had made up my mind: I must have one for myself.

Obviously the first thing I would have to do would be to move. A few days after I got back to New York I was deep in apartment-house plans.

Vincent Astor was at that time beginning work on the series of apartments which he had planned for East Eighty-sixth Street. They were to be the ultimate in apartments—I remember that they all featured solariums glassed with a product called "Vita-Glass," which, by permitting the actinic rays of the sun to penetrate them, assured you of a year-round tan without the necessity of moving out of town—and in exchange for a long-term lease it was possible to have them rather radically redesigned. The plan I finally evolved was certainly radical. It consisted of so rearranging the apartment that you came from the elevator directly into a thirty-foot-long gallery, which in turn continued into a living-room twenty-five feet wide. And there, fifty-five unobstructed feet away from the elevator door, with lighting designed to take the place of the skylight that even redesigning could not incorporate in a New York apartment house, would be the *Bird in Flight*, soaring away night and day in the general direction of the near-by German *Bierstuben*, with which East Eighty-sixth Street was lined for blocks. It was a stupendous task, and the renting agent seemed to approve of it highly. Probably the fact that people did not appear to be taking to the idea of paying high rents for the privilege of living in a neighborhood that had a tendency to smell like a brewery had something to do with his enthusiastic co-operation with my ideas.

In any case, nothing came of this scheme for the very simple reason that I soon discovered that I could not possibly afford to pay the rent involved. I regretfully dropped the whole project, including the purchase of the sculpture itself. But I was by then an accepted Brancusi connoisseur, and when the customs case came to court, I appeared and duly swore to the fact that the object on display in the courtroom was indeed a work of art of great value. So did a number of other witnesses who were called to testify. The government managed to produce two sculptors who testified that the object was neither a work of art nor a sculpture. But they were very much in the minority.

The judge considered the case carefully. "The piece," he said, "is characterized as a bird. However, it has neither head nor feet nor feathers, and without the exercise of rather a vivid imagination it bears no resemblance to a bird, except, perchance, that with such imagination it may be likened to the shape of the body of a bird. It must be conceded that what have been determined to be works of art under the decisions of recent years, would, under the more remote decisions of the courts, have been rejected as not falling within that term. There has been developing a so-called new school of art, whose exponents attempt to portray abstract ideas rather than to imitate natural objects. Whether or not we are in sympathy with these newer ideas, we think that the facts of their existence and their influence upon the art world must be considered." Brancusi's *Bird in Flight*, he ruled, was entitled to be admitted to the United States free of duty as a work of art. I had a feeling that he would have liked to have added: "and may God have mercy on this country's soul!"

My next excursion in the rarefied atmosphere of the upper reaches of æstheticism was a study in frustration. I became a devotee of Thomas Wilfred and his color organ the Clavilux. There, I decided, lay the true future of art. I would sit by the hour in his darkened studio watching the patterns of color roll out on the screen on which he projected them, clouds of deep red that would billow into ever lighter and lighter shades of that color, and then almost imperceptibly change to light yellow and blue and, in turn, every color of the spectrum. There were no designs in what he produced sitting at his keyboard. Or rather there were all the designs nature and man had ever created. Each session with the Clavilux was a unique experience, each wispy strand of color something to be remembered and savored.

But it was obvious that unless I were to build myself a theater in which to live, I could not hope to own one of his machines. And even if I did own one I could not possibly play it as he did. Having had no precedents to follow, he had designed the Clavilux to express his own ideas; in the hands of anyone else it lost most of its meaning. I tried to think of something I could do about it—a play perhaps, using the color organ instead of sets. But the Neighborhood Theater had had the same idea, and it had not proved too successful. I finally had to give up. And I have always been sorry about it. There have been many times when I would have liked to sit back again watching the astounding procession of colors unfold before me.

And then there was the time that I decided that George Antheil was the man to compose the first great American opera, and that Robinson Jeffers was the ideal choice as librettist. I did not meet him until many years later, but we had been corresponding for some time, ever since the first publication of his poetry by Boni & Liveright. I wrote him at once and asked him if he had ever thought of writing an opera. His answer came a few days later, and with it a two-page outline of his plan for a work entitled *The Song of Triumph*. He was most enthusiastic about the whole idea, he wrote, and he felt that the libretto he had in mind would lend itself perfectly to our purposes. Besides which, he pointed out, it would not be too difficult a production: all that was needed would be four singers and a chorus.

It was not exactly a cheerful opera he suggested. The world, he wrote, is desolate and dead. Wars, pestilences, famines, weariness of life—all these have taken their toll.

And not only is the earth dead, but other planets are too. When the earth failed, these other planets were colonized in a desperate attempt to save the human race, but for a thousand years now no ship or message has returned. But in a desert valley live Marah and her old father and mother, the sole human survivors on the earth. And to them comes Attis, Prometheus and Jesus reincarnate, mocked at by the dead for the failure of his promises and attempts.

That set the scene, and from there on it was pure Jeffers: Marah decides that her only hope of fruitfulness lies in Attis, but he resists her and finally mutilates himself and dies to avoid yielding to her. Next she turns to her father, but he is too old for her purposes. She builds a fire in the graveyard and begs the dead to fertilize her. But her father, imagining her pregnant, stabs her out of jealousy and then kills himself. And Marah dies of her wound, singing the song of the triumph of humanity, and only the old mother, gone mad, is left on earth.

I knew enough about opera to feel that this was not exactly what the Metropolitan was looking for at that time. I put the outline carefully away among my papers.

I ended the musical part of my æsthetic career on a thin, whiny note, the only sound that the Theremin would produce. I had been reading about this new instrument for some time, and I decided that I had to have one, and as soon as possible. My order was in for weeks before the first machine was ready for delivery. I barely listened to the instructions the salesman tried to give me before it was finally installed in my living-room. There was no reason for me to have to listen, I told myself. Here was obviously the easiest machine in the world to play. I could hardly wait for the installation to be completed.

Finally I stood before my Theremin, alone with it at last. On its tall, thin legs it very much resembled an old-fashioned bookkeeper's desk, with a metal loop extending from its right side, and a metal rod coming out of the top on the left. By moving one hand in relation to the rod, you produced electronic sounds that covered a wide range of the musical scale. In the meantime the other hand crawled snakewise at and through the loop, thereby controlling the volume of sound you were creating. In effect it was the radio manufacturers' answer to the meat packers' claim that they used all of the pig except the squeal. They were actually using it, for the Theremin was nothing more or less than an instrument designed to exploit commercially what the radio industry had had to contend with for so long: the fact that unless your radio was effectively shielded, it would squeal and shriek when your hand approached the dial.

I turned the machine on and waved my hands at it. And then I recoiled and thought it over for a while. The first sounds I had produced had been horrible: unearthly, bansheelike wails. I tried again, and again I stopped as quickly as I could. The sounds had not been so ear-piercing this time, but they had been completely deafening. After a few hours, during which I expected the building superintendent to appear with the police at any minute to remind me that this was not a licensed slaughterhouse, I had made the great discovery that I could actually play a reasonable facsimile of the *Pagan Love Song* on the thing. And even though I tried again and again to play something else in the months I kept it, the *Pagan Love Song* remained the only recognizable tune I could ever coax out of my beautiful Theremin.

It was an excellent party gambit though. It looked so ridiculously easy to play that everybody wanted to try it. And there they would stand, waving their hands madly, trying to control it, speaking to it finally as if that might make it cease its almost uncontrollable howling. Then they would sit down, defeated. The only person, as a matter of fact, who ever managed to produce real music on it was Ben Hecht. A skilled violinist, he could wave his hands at the Theremin and it would obey him. It wasn't very pretty music he made, but at least it was music—that is, if you are the kind of person who feels that a steam calliope is a musical instrument. I finally gave it away, so that I would never hear its ear-piercing shrillness again.

It wasn't only in the field of the arts that I fancied myself as a pioneer. Medicine too offered tempting new vistas. There was, for instance, my experience as a human guinea pig in the hands of Louis Berman, the truly brilliant author of *Glands Regulating Personality*. It was his thesis that the ductless glands were the prime motivating factors in human life, and he claimed to be able to deduce from a famous person's life exactly what his glandular imbalance had been. He made a pretty good case for his theory too, and many of the things he stated have become part of the present-day medical lore. But in those days he was finding it difficult to make converts. I set out to help him in whatever way I could.

And one of the ways in which I could be most helpful was in making available to his patient study all the famous people whom I knew and entertained. He would come to our parties and sit quietly in a corner studying Dreiser or Anderson or someone else equally well known, and when they had gone, he would tell us his opinion of them—from a glandular point of view of course. Later, when he decided to experiment in the fields of hypnotism, we would witness the spectacle of Berman at his most soothing and persuasive, trying to put his volunteer subject to sleep so as to be able to implant a post-hypnotic suggestion. And then we would all of us sit around, watching the time, holding our breaths, wondering if at the predetermined moment the now completely awake subject would feel the irresistible impulse to cross the room and pick out the volume of *Poems in Praise of Practically Nothing* that had been carefully planted beforehand as the third volume from the left on the second shelf of the bookcase next to the window nearest the pantry. We never ceased to be surprised at how often his subjects did exactly what they had been told to do.

When Berman suggested to me that he could take fifty pounds off me by means of a novel diet which he had in mind, supplemented, of course, by a liberal use of glandular injections and of fresh glands in capsule form, I immediately put myself completely in his hands. Here I felt was a great opportunity to further scientific research and to become case history number one in a book that would revolutionize the whole science of dietetics. For six months I religiously followed the diet he gave me—a diet that consisted of meat and fish and potatoes and starches and sweets exclusively, with no vegetables or fruits permitted in any form. After each huge meal I would swallow two enormous capsules, through the transparent walls of which I could see the outlines of the fresh glands they contained. I had to get these capsules weekly at Fraser's, the only druggist in town who made them up, and they had to be kept on the ice in our icebox. In addition I had to go to Berman's offices twice a week for injections of a very special glandular extract that he had had prepared for me. Otherwise I led my life exactly as I would have if I had not been on his diet, which meant that the sum total of my exercising consisted of beckoning for the nearest taxi even if my destination was only three blocks away.

I weighed two hundred and twenty pounds when I went on the diet. After six months of lunches that consisted of huge plates of noodles, swimming in butter and topped with mounds of sour cream, and of dinners that began with lentil soup, continued through a thick steak with the largest baked potato obtainable, into which had been inserted roughly a quarter pound of butter, and ended with two or three helpings of chocolate soufflé, I had, to the complete amazement of my friends, lost almost fifty-five pounds. And that I decided was enough. I felt wonderfully well, and for the first time since my preadolescence days I was definitely not fat. But my clothes did not fit me any more, and besides I was getting tired of the biweekly visits to Berman's offices.

Six months later I crossed the two-hundred-pound mark again. I have stayed there ever since then. Without the constant input of glands, which tended to establish their own form of glandular imbalance, the diet Berman gave me proved worse than useless. And I came to realize that unless I wanted to be as dependent on this form of medication as any diabetes patient is on his Insulin, I could not hope ever again to be as thin as I had been when I went back to more normal eating. I have never regretted the choice I made. The thing that bothered me was that Berman abandoned his theories of diet after his experiment on me, and I never did become a case history in the book he had planned to write.

There was only one thing I managed to avoid in those years. I did not start a little magazine. But I did collect them avidly. In fact I collected all manner of first editions avidly. And it was not only because the mania for modern first editions was in full flower; I was on the inside and I enjoyed backing my judgment. I did pretty well at it too. I built up a really exciting library that at one time contained first editions of just about every important book published since the turn of the century.

Naturally I had among my books complete runs of first editions of Ronald Firbank and Norman Douglas and Aldous Huxley and A. E. Coppard and T. F. Powys and Arthur Machen and H. L. Mencken. No self-respecting collector of the twenties would have been without these books, or without the works of Carl Van Vechten and James Branch Cabell and D. H. Lawrence and Humbert Wolfe. And there were on my groaning shelves first-edition copies of *Zuleika Dobson* and *The Way of All Flesh* and *Of Human Bondage* and the *Spoon River Anthology*. All of them were very definitely mint copies, and most of them had their original dust wrappers. And in every one of the thousands of books that lined my walls from ceiling to floor I had pasted my own bookplate, a reproduction of a caricature Covarrubias had made of me in 1924. I thought this the height of sophistication.

But I soon found that collecting first editions in the usual way was merely a matter of watching catalogues, ordering the books I wanted, and then paying for them. That began to pall after a while. It was shortly after I had blocked off one of the doors leading to my kitchen to make room for another series of bookcases that I pulled my first real coup.

I was in the Holliday Bookshop one day in 1924 when I happened to pick up an English edition of a slim volume of poetry by A. A. Milne. *When We Were Very Young* was the title of the book, and as I read it I became convinced that here was the most delightful book of children's verses since Robert Louis Stevenson's *A Child's Garden of Verse*. I bought all the copies Holliday would sell me, and then I went around to the other booksellers and bought up their copies too. I found that the English publishers had issued a special autographed edition limited to one hundred copies, and I managed to pick up two copies from unsuspecting American dealers, who sold them to me at the regular price of twelve and a half dollars. And then I cabled to England and got three sets of all the issues of *Punch* in which these poems had originally appeared. After that I sat back and waited for the market to catch up to me.

It did. I had managed to assemble some twenty copies

of the regular English first edition, for which I had paid two dollars apiece. I sold them individually and over a period of time at thirty-five dollars apiece. The limited editions I sold for two hundred and seventy-five dollars each. Even the copies of *Punch*, tastefully cased, brought up to thirty dollars the set. And the copies of the American first edition, which I had bought just to see what would happen, brought twice to three times their published price.

I may have lost my standing as an amateur æsthete by this move, but I didn't care. My next maneuver was in connection with the first two Hemingway books, two privately printed pamphlets in editions of about one hundred copies each. I managed to get five copies of one of them and four of the other one, and I paid the regular price of a dollar and a half apiece for them. Less than five years later I sold them for two hundred and fifty dollars apiece.

And so it went. I combined my interest in new writers I might be able to discover with the even more practical pursuit of securing copies of their earliest work before their more mature creations had made these juvenilia collector's items. I was wrong a great number of times. Whatever happened to Leroy Macleod or to Charles Malam or H. Phelps Putnam or Lancelot de Giberne Sieveking? And who today reads Humbert Wolfe and James Hanley and Stephen Hudson and Robert McAlmon? But I was right often enough to succeed in assembling the most exciting amateur's library I have ever seen. At one point it consisted of almost ten thousand items, including hundreds of fugitive pamphlets, a robust collection of erotica all bound in red morocco, uncounted stacks of catalogues, complete runs of the publications of all the great contemporary presses, every art-gallery announcement for almost fifteen years, and almost a thousand issues of the various little magazines that were published over that same period of time.

I sold about a third of this collection at a two-session

auction at the Anderson Galleries in 1928, a little more than a year before the market crash. The fact that a copy of Will Durant's *Story of Philosophy* brought twenty-one dollars is indicative of the prices I obtained for the really important books offered in that sale. And during the course of the next few years I sold my complete runs of Dreiser and James Stephens and Robinson Jeffers and T. S. Eliot and James Joyce and Edna St. Vincent Millay, and all the other complete collections I had managed to assemble, at prices that would seem fantastically high today. In 1935 when I sold out all my remaining first editions my library was still important enough for me to be able to sell it to R. H. Macy and Company, who started a rare book shop with my collection as a base and issued a first catalogue that included such items as a signed copy of Elinor Wylie's *Jennifer Lorn* for fifteen dollars and ninety-seven cents, and a copy of *Emperor Jones*, illustrated by Alexander King, for six dollars and forty-nine cents.

And yet when I went through the complete list of my collection a short while ago, I could find less than a hundred books I would like to own today. The passion for possessions, which was such an important part of the life of the young æsthete of the twenties, long ago became a thing of the past. It began to die with the crash, when we first became aware of the impermanence of everything we had thought of as timelessly safe. It passed out of our lives completely in the hard days of the depression. And after the uprooting of our lives in the war years it is hard to imagine any of us ever building our lives again around the importance of owning a mint copy of Richard Hughes's *Lines Written on First Observing an Elephant Devoured by a Roc*, a four-page pamphlet printed for the author by the Golden Cockerel Press in an edition of twenty-five copies, numbered and autographed by the author.

NINETEEN

IT WASN'T MUCH FUN

Aᴼ ᶠᵉᵂ months ago I finished writing a novel about the twenties. It was, as I have said before, very bad. But what astonished me most about it was that in writing a story that was as honest as I could make it I also wrote one that turned out to be almost completely horizontal. The succession of rumpled sheets, tumbled couches, and parked cars was staggering. My characters seemed to have little time for anything but continuous, casual rolls in the hay.

I showed this novel to some old friends, realists all, people who had lived through the whole silly period with me. They were horrified. They had never, they assured me, had experiences similar to the ones I wrote about. Theirs had been an idyllic life, full of moonlight and honeysuckle, rich with remembered moments of ecstasy. Of course, I agreed with them hastily; this book was not about them. They were different. I had written about the other people in our lives. They smiled their gratitude. They seemed completely satisfied. And for the next hour or so they wallowed in an orgy of sentimental reminiscences. To listen to them one would have thought that the good old twenties were the greatest period in the world's history.

But then to almost everybody, memories of the twenties are pure nostalgia, a series of beautiful pictures in beautiful rich frames. Remember, they will say, and their faces will light up, and they will go on blissfully reliving their departed youth. Or at least that is what they think they are doing. Actually it is nothing of the sort.

It is mostly material things they are remembering with such fatuous joy. And there can be no denying that those things were simpler then. Did you want to go to Europe? You had your choice of cabins on ten ships. Did you want a new car? It was wisest not to let this be known too loudly or you would be deluged with salesmen, all extolling their own make of car, all offering you long demonstration rides into the country. Did you want to move? Your real-estate broker would oblige with page after page of listings, and the landlord of your final choosing would do his best to have the repainting you had ordered match the sample of material you had given him as a guide.

Of course all of these things are out of the question now. It is no longer possible to run away from oneself by getting on a cruise ship or going to Europe or moving into a new apartment. And the one fact that most of us who lived through those fantastic years do not realize is that running away was exactly what we were doing. We ran from reality. We ran from the horrible possibility of being alone with our thoughts and the realization that our lives were empty and sterile and meaningless. We ran from the even more harrowing truth that we had become disillusioned with our own disillusionment and that we were suddenly faced with the probability that there was no point in doing anything at all. We ran from everything all the time.

So we kept on the go constantly, and we had the widest choice of amusement that has ever been offered any generation. The world was very definitely our oyster, and we knew it. The vogues, the fads, the crazes that followed each other in bewildering succession, were all devised for our enjoyment. Sometimes it seemed as if fully half of the world was performing solely to entertain us.

Between the turn of the century and the beginning of the thirties the world changed so completely that nothing was ever the same again. In those few years automobiles, telephones, airplanes, radio, and motion pictures came from nowhere to become integral parts of our lives. Distances melted away, and natural barriers disappeared. And in the immediate future loomed such things as supersonic planes and atom bombs and all the other marvels science has evolved to give us pause, to make us stop and consider the monsters we have created for our own destruction. But we weren't aware of these facts then. Far from it. To us everything that was being done was for the increase of our creature comforts. It never occurred to us that science had any other purpose.

Actually we were very much unaware. We rarely read the papers, and when we did it was to read about sports and plays and scandal. We read only those among the serious books that dealt with personal problems. We tried to pretend that there was no world except the very narrow one of our own invention. We chose to ignore the fact that somewhere outside our immediate orbit a great mass of very simple people continued to lead their very simple lives. Or rather we chose to laugh at these poor ignorant ones. They were yokels, they were boobs, they were old-fashioned. They were everything that we pitied. And the fact that they pitied us quite as much was a source of constant incredulous amusement to us.

I listen when people talk about the twenties, and I don't

say anything. I lived those years fully, and I did everything that everybody did, and many things that they never got around to doing. And I would not go back to the life we led then for anything in the world. I honestly do not think that we had very much fun, no matter what we did, for we were living in a cheap and shoddy world, in which the desperate search for pleasure was mistaken for pleasure itself.

It came about quite naturally, I suppose. In our revolt against the Victorian codes of conduct we had taken the anarchistic stand that the only sound code was no code at all. "Be honest with one's self," was one credo. And that, to most people, meant to permit one's self to do anything one wanted to. There was a corollary to this. "Never do anything that hurts anyone else," it stated. And that presupposed frankness carried to the point where all pleasure staled. The unexpected moment of time was most effectively killed off by this last bit of specious thinking.

I lived my life at the hub of the period. The spokes went out in all directions, but they stemmed from the things I did, or at least from the things that people immediately about me did. Every school of thought, if it could be dignified by the use of the word "thought," every moment in art, in music, in literature, grew out of the ideas of people with whom I was in constant and intimate contact. And I absorbed their ideas like a sponge. We were the pioneers. We were the innovators. The world would gratefully accept the new directions we had surveyed for them. The future was ours to mold. Of all this we were absolutely certain.

And being certain of these things, we knew other things too. We knew that a silly fad, devised in a moment of alcoholic boredom, could become an accepted pastime, that we had but to put the stamp of our approval on any concept of morality for it to be hailed as a further step in the direction of escape from the fettering past. We lived in a world obsessed with the need for breaking away from everything that had been held to be right, and we were obsessed in as full a measure with the need of showing the way toward that goal. The results were just slightly less than catastrophic.

It wasn't so much that we lived a life of senseless and constant pleasure. It wasn't so much that we escaped from every vaguest need to fulfill our obligations. It wasn't even that we came to deny the fact that we had any obligations. It was rather that because of our basic ignorance, because of the fact that we had not been educated to think about the world or politics or the broader aspects of anything, we thought of nothing but ourselves and the immediate orbit that revolved about us. We were showing the way to the rest of the world, and the fact that we had absolutely no idea of where we were going bothered us not at all.

Which is why I repeat that the twenties were not much fun. With the whole world and all its resources at our disposal, we frittered away all the wonderful things that were bountifully poured out in front of us. And the tragedy of it all was that we did not know what we were doing. I can think of nothing more depressing than to remember all the things we could have done with this enormously exciting world, and then to realize how we wasted our last chance to enjoy it.

There was, for instance, sex. Probably no generation was ever as sex-conscious as we were. It was almost as if we had invented the whole thing. We fought for the right to live our sexual life as we chose to. We battled to discard the shackles of Victorian morality. We cast off the fetters of convention and broke the handcuffs of monogamistic thinking. And then we tried to kindle a fire from these discarded impediments, and to fan it into life with the breath of our hot and impassioned arguments. We failed miserably.

There has probably never been a time in the history of modern man when sex was less enjoyable.

For after a while it ceased to be much more than obligatory, and nothing that could have happened could have had a more depressing result. The constant need on the part of men to bolster their waning egos with horizontal successes, the equally constant need of women to assert their emancipation by arrogating to themselves privileges that had previously been entirely and particularly male—these conflicting compulsions made for a perpetual rutting season of singular dullness. There was not even any pretense of affection involved, no irresistible urge of male body toward female body, of man toward woman. It became a coupling of any man with any woman, and the changing of partners in the stylized sexual dance was as obligatory as the changing of the guard at Buckingham Palace.

Naturally this sexual round dance had its effect on the marriages of the period. I can think of only one of them that managed to survive the buffetings of the cult of freedom. The others melted away in a kaleidoscopic pageant of affairs, divorces, remarriages—and then affairs, divorces, and remarriages again. "Monogamy" was an ugly word to us in those days. It was the cake that was offered to the masses. For us there was the tasty bread of license.

There was some reason for this feeling on our part. It was a hangover from our adolescent fear of being considered old-fashioned. And that, in our minds, was the equivalent of being called prudish. And that in turn was an insult we would do anything to avoid. No truly emancipated girl in the twenties, for instance, would ever admit to being a virgin. No matter how she felt about it, no matter how pure her thoughts, she knew that she must invent some plausible story as an explanation of her unfortunate state. And she also knew that if she expected to be accepted as a modern, she would soon have to take the necessary steps to correct this condition.

Who, with this life as his whole motivation, could expect to savor any part of it fully? Obviously it became necessary to invent a series of diversions ranging from crossword puzzles to the specious excitement of Channel swimmers to keep from realizing how meaningless everything was. And even then one rarely succeeded. Which is probably why the anesthesia of alcohol was such a welcome escape for so many people. The wonder is that so many others managed to avoid it.

It was when the beautiful red carpet was rudely pulled out from under our feet in the thirties that we came to see life as it really was. And there were many of us who could not face its ugly reality. For too long a time had we lived in a musical-comedy world with a musical-comedy cast of characters. The sudden shift to drama, and drama that demanded of us that we play our parts seriously, found us unprepared to shoulder our responsibilities. We floundered about, completely out of our element, trying everything we could think of to escape from the inescapable world. And it was only when we came to accept the fact that we were actually parts of this world that we found our release. We found it in many ways, each according to his fashion, and we took up our newly found duties with reluctance. It was not for some years that we finally realized that we were really living for the first time in our lives.

And of course the prewar years, and the war itself, and the precarious world we are living in today, all helped us to adjust ourselves and to regain our balance. We had no choice in the matter. The world was too much with us, and it was no longer possible to ignore it. Besides which, and most importantly, we had become aware of it. The books we read, the newspapers, the magazines, the things we listened to on the air—all these reduced us as individuals to our rightful proportions. With impending chaos as our daily companion, it was no longer possible for us to think of ourselves as islands in a placid sea.

Besides which we were growing older. We began to lack the energy for some of the pastimes that had seemed such an essential part of our lives. And others, repeated too often over a period of too many years, staled and became meaningless. And the specter of lonely old age, while it did not exactly stand at our shoulders, still began to enter into our consciousness every now and then. That, above all, was the most sobering thought. It made us realize finally how empty and directionless our lives had been. And we took what steps we could to correct these facts. After a while we came to realize that somehow, and almost in spite of ourselves, we had grown up. But of one thing we would always be certain. The life we had led had been no help to us in this painful process.

I know these things at first hand. I lived them as fully as I lived the twenties. I know how hard it was to throw off the ideas and habits I had formed. It was a battle every step of the way, and one for which I was ill fitted. But I like to think that I have won it. I would not have it otherwise. Certainly I hope that I am not like that couple who were, as was I, products of the twenties, and who to this day have made no attempt to change their ways. They live their lives as if Joe Smith were still playing for tea dances in the Plaza Grill, and they almost seem to be carrying invisible flasks under imaginary coonskin coats. They were at a party a short while back, and their host stood their childish antics as long as he could. But finally he reached the breaking point. "Go away," he said. "Go home you—you—you fugitives from F. Scott Fitzgerald. Go home and grow up."

INDEX

INDEX

iv

A NOTE ON THE TYPE IN WHICH
THIS BOOK IS SET

Waverley, the type used in this book, is a new design produced by the Intertype Corporation. Named for Captain Edward Waverley, the hero of Sir Walter Scott's first novel, it is inspired by the spirit of Scott's literary creation rather than actually derived from the typography of that period. Indeed, Waverley is a wholly modern typeface, if not by definition, certainly by association with the designs of our best contemporary typographers.

The book was composed, printed, and bound by H. Wolff, New York. The typography and binding were designed by Marshall Lee.